LIVE

NOW

How I Found Purpose, Love,
and Healing in the Face of a
Terminal Illness

Russell K. Symmes
with Louisa M. Percudani

Mosaic Publishing LLC
ISBN: 987-0-578-59188-9

I have tried to recreate events, locales and
conversations from my memories of them. In order
to maintain their anonymity in some instances I
have changed the names of individuals and places,
I may have changed some identifying character-
istics and details such as physical properties, occu-
pations and places of residence.

Printed in the United States of America.

DEDICATION

For Russ Symmes
In memoriam August 24, 1958 – December 11, 2002
Thank you for showing me how to live brilliantly and
courageously in the moment.

For Ken and Norma Symmes

CONTENTS

Introduction

Everything matters now. You want to know how to navigate all this uncertainity. How to wrap your mind—no, your life—around this. You or your loved one has just gotten the call, or just left the doctor's office—it's cancer.

For Russ Symmes, known by many as "The Big Kahuna," a nickname given while an offensive tackle for Arizona State University, the last thing he expected while traveling in Paris was that his cancer would come in the form of a grand-mal seizure. He had ignored the pounding headaches. He was used to working through pain and stress. He was thirty-three, married and a successful executive.

He arrived back in the States to a doctor's diagnosis of death. A rare, orange-sized tumor—an oligodendroglioma astrocytoma—had taken up residence in the temporal lobe of his brain. Surgery held the promise extending his life for a month, or at the most three. He had come face-to-face with his biggest opponent and there was no way he was going to back down.

He began simply by seizing the day. He would have to learn to walk, talk, and read again. He trusted his doctors at

Barrow Neurological Institute and also sought out alternative therapies to heal his mind, body, and soul.

Russ lived for ten and half more years. He continued to thrive on his own road as he rebuilt his life. His marriage ended and his career needed to be reinvented. He inspired many newly-diagnosed cancer patients with his love and courage. His daily creed: Carpe Diem.

In 1995 he met me, his future wife, at a Christmas party. It wasn't until the Spring of 2000, though, that a chance meeting at a bookstore led us to confess a deep love for each other. Russ proposed three months later, and we were married the following Spring.

Six months before he died, he started writing and putting the poems in a unique order. Over the years, he had written them on scrap paper, paper bags, corners of newspapers, and anything he could find when he felt drawn to release. He intimately shared his hopes, desires, and moments of despair as he navigated the pain of divorce, the memories of the past, and the uncertainty of his future. He asked me to add our love story, and the beauty of life's unexpected gifts.

Russ's wish was that his story would inspire all of us to never give up. No matter what you are facing today, may his journey fill you with love, hope, and inspiration.

-- Louisa M. Percudani

I Might Die

Russ

There is only so much you can do to get your emotions and head ready for surgery. I don't remember feeling scared, just uneasy because everyone around me was sad and upset.

The day before surgery, I tried not to think about what would happen if I died. It still went through my mind no matter how hard I tried. What would it feel like? Where would I go? Have I done anything to send me to hell? I know I had not been perfect over the years. What about dying and going to heaven? From all I've learned in church, I felt pretty comfortable about heaven, and it sure seemed like the right time to attend now. There is no easy way to contemplate life and death, the future, or all the possible changes that could take place.

My parents and my wife (at the time) drove me to Barrow Neurological Institute in Phoenix that morning. Slowly, with the process of checking in, paperwork, and plastic wrist-bands, the reality of what was about to happen began to phase into my emotions. I tried so hard to keep steady within my mind. I was ready to play this game, not just for myself, but for all the "football fans" that were there.

I was assigned my own little room and then instructed to change into my special hospital gown. It was simple and embarrassing, too. For me, it was a bit tight and short for my 245-lb, muscular 6'6" frame. I was asked to lay down on the hospital bed and relax. *"Yeah, like you can really relax."*

And then roll call started. People came in to introduce themselves and peppered me with questions – allergies, medicines, etc. I would be awake for the nine-hour brain-mapping surgery. The next step was fun: a haircut. I got to say goodbye to all the hair on my head, but they let me keep my full beard.

It was time to move on to the surgical room, and I began my ride down the hallway. As we arrived in front of the big surgical doors, I saw my family and my friend, Pastor Staats.

I think we all tried to reinforce our love and feelings that everything was going to be all right. I could see so much in the eyes of my parents. I felt them both with me, inside my heart. Before they rolled me in, I got to say a prayer, last rights, with Pastor Staats. It brought me into the reality of what was about to take place and I could feel it. There was some safety, some fear, a mixture of shock. I might die. (It's really hard to put this down on paper.) As the big doors opened, I felt I was drifting away from reality into another part of the planet only the special get to go to. I just wished I was pushing the gurney instead of riding on it.

It was a whole other world in there. Equipment of all kinds surrounded me. Only the surgical team's spectacle-covered eyes stared at me, as they were outfitted in special gowns. I hung way over the surgical table and giggles filled the room, which – oddly – made me feel a little more comfortable.

The head nurse said, "You are going to feel some warmth going into your arm and travel up your vein. You'll get a taste in your mouth and feel really tired. We will all start to fade and look like we are drifting away. You will go unconscious. When you are established, I will bring you back into consciousness, but you will feel good and comfortable."

I anticipated the drugs. *Will it feel like the first time I got drunk or stoned?* An ice cube of cold burst into my veins with heat into my arm and then with freeway speed into my head. A sharp, gasoline-smelling fluid filled every crevice of my nose and mouth. I started to spin around like a car out of control into a very strange world. I heard voices and then I was gone.

The next thing I remembered was the doctor asking how I felt. Everyone was within sight, although I didn't know exactly what they were doing. I felt comfortable. Dr. Fisher started talking to me. He asked me, "What is your name?" And I res-ponded, "Russ Symmes." Then they moved the pin. He asked me, "What state are you in?" I responded in a blurry way: "Arrrilliz arrr." Then they moved the pin. He asked me, "What's your mother's name?" I responded, "Norma." Then they marked it so they would not take that part of my brain out.

This procedure is called intraoperative brain mapping, or awake brain surgery. It allowed my surgeon to remove the tumor without damaging other parts of my brain.

I can still visualize the surgery in front of my face. I have had a lot dreams about it. I have had no control over the feeling it created. I have jumped out of bed, soaking wet because I believed I was on the table again.

The next thing I felt or saw made me sick to my stomach. I really lost it. The intensity of pain inside of my head was magnified with a feeling of being twisted and off base. It took a long time to understand what had happened. People didn't look normal. I could hear them but they didn't make sense. As I awoke more and more, I started to realize what had happened. I felt like a little kid being taken care of by his mother.

I remembered seeing my family for a very short time. After I was fully stabilized, they took me up to my room.

Recovering was my next scene on the stage, and it was a journey of every emotion in the world. A feeling I had never experienced before came deep inside my heart as I passed a cross on the way back to my room. I felt comfort and safety. My life had changed. I had a mission, but I didn't know what it was yet.

So you have a chunk of your brain gone and have to re-route the pathways as you relearn all the basics: talk, read, write, add. The hard part is you don't know what's gone or how to start, or how bad the damage is.

It was difficult to pick up a book and stare at a word, again and again. I knew I had seen it before, but something was not connecting. I pronounced it letter by letter, opened my mouth and tried to sound it out, but it still wouldn't register. I would skip the word and keep reading, hoping the sentence would make sense. I hid my problems from people by pretending everything was fine.

Going from owning your own business to the equivalent of starting your very first job again, like when you were a kid, is not very much fun on your ego. I applied for a job at a gym to begin my life two years after surgery. It was not easy because I knew some of the people who worked out there and they remembered me as an intelligent, rich, business owner. I was so embarrassed so deep inside it was hard to hold my head up or look them in the eye.

How do I explain what had happened without driving myself crazy? Will they reject me, feel sorry for me and treat me like a child? Everyone was different. For the most part people were kind, but it was still a constant battle with my ego with new disabilities. Inside my heart and soul, I had to fight every day just to build my pride. It was the biggest first step I had taken back into the real world, but it was worth it. What a way to learn the reality of life!

As time went by, I was able to rebuild friendships, although nothing was the same. Dealing with such changes is hard to understand. In some ways you remember your past, in other ways you compare your changes by what people tell you, or by pictures you see that make you wonder. Looking back, I remember the depression I felt while I was relearning.

People need to look at their lives in a positive way. Period. The support I got from my family helped me more than ever. But it is up to you to move on with your head up. Don't compare yourself with anyone else. We are all unique. Period. Live on your own road, not on the road everyone lives on. Being "unique" is a positive part of living now. Don't try to be that person you used to be.

I read them
I write them
I think about them
Poems
They do help me
They release my emotions you see
They don't rhym
all the time
and my spelling is intertwined
But It helps
So I continue
to your heart is within you
Healing your feeling
Poems
They revealing

The Good, the Bad, and the Ugly

Russ

Something made me start writing poems. To release stress. They came out of my hands without thought. I would just pick up a piece of paper and a pen and write. The original poems were written on scrap paper, bags of paper, corners of newspaper – anything I could find when I felt drawn to release. Some have dates. Some don't. Some have titles. Some just have a comment or number. Over time they seem to get longer and more detailed.

It started when my now ex-wife asked me to move out of our newly-built house to give her some space and some time to think about life and our marriage.

The movie, *The Good, the Bad, and the Ugly* in many ways describes what can take place in your life when you think you are happily married. Lose your business and find your wife cheating, while you're fighting terminal cancer. Your mate is still willing to help you in any way, but does not want to be together anymore. Wow. What a slap in the face. Reality. Here you are recovering from your brain surgery and mind damage, only to have it crushed.

What an unbelievable personal downhill impact! In my case, I had just enough control to file for the divorce myself, present the legal form in a strong stance, to demand what I felt was fair, to present the evidence I found and to control my heart in one hell of an emotional presentation.

I felt remorse, hate, and confusion after that emotional event. I wondered if it was the right thing to do. I had some heart-wrenching ups and downs in what was left of my mind.

A big glass picture of Jesus hung in a church behind my house at that time. I would sit in front of him and break into tears like I had never done before, asking God what I should do in my life now. How can I get over this heartbreaking, emotionally crushing, life-changing smack in the face?

Big Step Up

Just having my lunch today
Thinking about the sport we play
Human beings seem to try to win
They search
They cheat
They steal
They make up answers
They even sin
What does it take
To be happy with your life
Should the team be
The husband and wife
Or just the friends and family
We already have
I guess we need a coach or something or somebody
That can see all sides
So we love ourselves – smile
And keep our pride
RS 10-22-94 (I wrote this on an Arby's bag)

Time Change

Just a minute
How does time go by so fast
When you want it to slow down
Just a second
What time is it now?
The clock went by
Where was I?
Then, when you are uncomfortable
the clock slows down
How does it know
To go so slow
To make you think
Tick - Tick - Tick
RS 10-28-94

Divorce Is a Source

Of course that is coarse
RS '94

3/43-155

You split up to be happy
Yet it still turns out to be crappy
RS '94

Climbing Up

How in the hell
Do I get used to all the changes
It was hard enough
To go from the single, wide open countryside
To the bumpy married ranges
Now it's a mountain
Starting all over again
I just want to know;
Do I wait at the bottom?
Climb to the top
Or walk up the path
And see who I might bump into*
RS Oct. 28, 1994
** I think about this now and my wife Louisa jumps into my
heart and says YES! 8-13-00*

3/43 – 157

Divorce, Recovery
Discovery of my life
RS '94

Craving Tears

At my desk doing bills
Writing letters, writing Will
All alone, making plans
Good Story
You can be King or Queen,
Rich or poor
Fat or skinny
And you are still a human
On the planet earth
Make the most of it
A day at a time
If you think about all the good things versus the bad
You will and the good one lasts longer much stronger
Read it
Believe it
RS 10-28-94

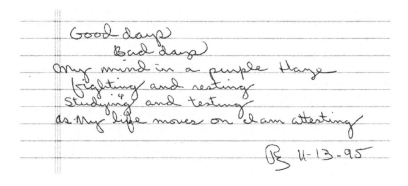

Good days)
    Bad days)
My mind in a purple Haze
Fighting and resting
Studying and testing
as My life moves on I am attesting
                    RS 11-13-95

It Will Get Better

Today was a day
When my emotions had to pay
My feelings
My life
Memories of my X-wife...
Changes can hurt
Life sometimes is painful
You can smile
You can frown
You can feel up or down
But we can't ever give up
So moments like this
Make you miss a kiss a hug
That loving look, that warm feeling...
Now we are cold
A blanket can help
Your cat or dog, you can hug and share love
RS 10-28-94

Life Goes On, and On, and On

Enjoy it while you can
POSITIVE ATTITUDE REQUIRED!
RS 11-94

Goodbye to Them

Why did I write this poem?
I guess I miss my home
I miss my wife
I miss my life
Don't forget her Mom and Dad
They are still your friends and family
Even though you don't talk to them anymore
RS 11-4-94

Ink Release

Sometimes I write these
Just to let it out
To release my sorrow
My stress
My anger
My broken heart
Gee... I wish they would fix everything too
RS 11-4-94

3/31 – 125

Hey You!
There is a happy side
Life moves on
Smiles come back
RS 11-94

Lonely Poemly

You are only lonely
when you meet someone nice
You are only lonely
when you think about yourself
You are only lonely
when you write a poem about it
RS

Fade Away

There was a trace on her face
On the lady
She was shady
There was a lump
in my heart
as she walked away
The lump and the trace went to space...
RS

Vote

I voted yesterday
Had nothing to say
It's up to you to lead the way
... OK
RS 11-9-94

Game Tied

How do you stop your memory
How can I forget?
Can You? Should You? Will You?
When you leave although you really don't want to
but have to, then what?
When the other has committed the crime
You lose...
They lose...
Everyone loses...
RS

Past vs. Future

Why do we keep thinking about our past
Worrying about the future
When we should be living one day at a time?
RS 11-9-94

Put 'Ur Up

On the way to my life
I was told all about the husband and wife
I was told that's the way we survive
No one mentioned the battle
RS 11-94

Fix It Please

NOW
Right NOW
I can't wait any longer
My love has gotten stronger
... OOPS
Reality has actually damaged it
Broken it
Made it protect itself
I hope it's OK
I pray it can start working again
RS 12-9-94

Something's Burning

We were impalpable
I was impelled
You were impatient
I was imperfect
Our marriage incinerated
RS 12-94

Wacked Once Again

Here's a poem that struck me out
It started suddenly
With a yelling shout
A piece of paper
With former facts
Of a previous life
Now causing cracks in my head
in my heart
I wish I had not seen them
It reminded me of our past
RS 12-9-94

Damn My Memory

Here I am
Thinking of you again
Reminiscing
Getting pissed off
Missing you too much
Upset since it's Christmas
Lonely
How do I celebrate this year
Or next year
Or the year after that...
RS 12-20-94

Just having my lunch today
Thinking about the sport we play
Human beings seem to try to win
They search
 They cheat
  They steal
 They make up answers
  They even sin.
what does it take
  To be happy with your life
Should the team be
  The husband and the wife?
 or just the friends & family
    we already have
~~that are ~~

 I guess we need a coach
That sees all sides   *a something /
            a somebody/
So we love ourselves - smile
  and keep our pride

R 10-12-94

Why Did This Happen To Me?

Russ

Why did this happen to me?
There is no cancer in my family. I don't think I deserved brain cancer. I mean, what did I do wrong? When did it start living in my body? Where does it come from? How many different cancers are there? How do doctors know what is going to happen to us?

Questions, questions and more questions... and there are really are no perfect answers. But the good side of the story is that we are learning more every day.

I am a lucky one, still living despite the percentages. Why? I think there are several reasons why and I want to share them with everyone.

- The things you need to know and not forget are:
- We all have different bodies.
- We all have different kinds of cancer at different stages.
- We all have cancer in different places in our bodies.

- We all have different bodies and brains so we react differently to everything.
- We all react to medicine, surgery, and radiation treatment differently.
- We all think differently.
- We all react differently to what the doctor tells us.
- We all will find different doctors that have different ideas and backgrounds.
- We all have different families and friends around us who react in a million different ways.
- We all have different religious or spiritual beliefs. Or we don't believe in anything.
- We all go through a series of reactions – from anger, fear, hate, confusion, craziness, pain, suffering, changing, and then acceptance.
- We all don't think it is fair that it happened to us.
- We all become sad about what we will miss in our lives.
- We all hate what we are doing to our family because they are suffering with us.
- We all want to find a way out of the pain we suffer.
- We all could add so much to this list.

Think about what you just read. You could basically understand what I meant. But how can we make fighting and beating cancer more positive? What does it take? Where do we begin? How can I do the right thing?

The first step is a positive attitude. Period. Whether you're the one with cancer or part of the family. You have to look at the positive side. I know everyone has heard it before, but it really makes a difference. Think of the positive things you can do.

You can find new ways to heal yourself, like vitamins, minerals, supplements.

You can find different ways to keep physically in shape – walking, running, light to heavy weight lifting, creative workouts, hiking, biking, climbing in the mountains, trotting on a beach, yoga classes. Try anything carefully.

You can change what you eat.

You can go to a variety of alternative medicine practitioners: naturopaths, acupuncturists, yogis, reikis, just to name a few.

You can find support groups, pray with groups, meditate, visualize, or seek out cancer hotlines.

You can take a friend with you and make it a fun learning experience.

You can take classes that will help you keep a positive attitude at a local college.

You can change your attitude by reading stories about people who have learned to beat cancer and get your spirit in a positive mode.

You can think of new ways to better your life by keeping a positive attitude, all the time, especially when you are talking with your doctor.

*Next four were written in Pinetop, I was by myself:

Need Some Changes

My eyes are sad today
I did not plan on being down
Someone else made me realize
I am alone now
I have to start all over again
Where do I go
Where do I look
Why...
How do I move on
How do I keep a smile on my face
When do I feel good again
RS 1995

A Moment In the Hill

In the darkness of the night
And the chill in the air
I was alone having dinner
Trying to figure out how to care
How do I focus on the feeling in my heart
All that confusion
Is that an illusion?
Do I see love in the air
There is something. Or is there?
It will take some time to not crack
Somehow life will come back
RS 1-6-95

I Can Hear Now

There is a look
There is a sound
My feelings begin to abound
There is humor
There is care
There is a mystery in the air
The future may have been resolved
RS 1-6-95

Is That What I Saw?

Did I see her?
Did I feel it?
A look in her eyes
What a surprise
There was a positive feeling
For real... or memory...?
RS 1-6-95

Religion is like a pegion
There are many differnt
                    Kinds
But they all can fly
    up to the sky
Some flow smoothly
    others cruise
then many follow a pattern,
    a schedule, then snoony
But, no matter how you view
    the flight
what you believe in
    will help you win the fight

8-5-95

A Glance In My Eye

I may be someone
from another place
But I want you to know
the happy look you put on my face
Becoming single after many years
has been a fight
to hold back the tears
You somehow made good feelings start
My heart began to beat
My feelings realized reality
There are wonderful people out there
You are the one that will
help me dream again
Thank you for being special
You've made me find out
Love is potential and essential
RS 1 -6-95
* *Skiing by myself, I wrote this while having dinner alone, when a woman walked by and glanced at me. Just one second of eye contact made me feel better.*

Last Payment

Payments are made
For mistakes we have paid
Last checks are written
Last thoughts released
Last memories erased
Last Love in our heart
Last feeling in depth
I guess I came in last
RS 2-95

Get My Money Back

Oh was the day so clear
I realized she would never be here
The final last step was made
Names were removed, the last bill was paid
That ring that I got her, I sent the last check in
And then I tried to forget her
Hey! Can I get a refund?
RS 2-3-95

Steal It All

You have a birthday – holding
Feelings floating
Life unfolding
Pressure unloading
Happiness croaking
Past - only you can remember
Future – I use to be a member
I barely made it thru December
Now I recollect and recall
Is this what you wanted
And why you took it all
RS 2-8-95

Down Goes the Poem

You would think after all of this
That all I missed about you was your kiss
Or perhaps it was just your look
That special face
Why is my whole life out of place?
Where is yours now
Are you happy as can be
Is it everything you wanted to be
Do you ever think about me?
Just writing this made me sad as can be
RS 2-6-95

Rhyming

I read them
I write them
I think about them
POEMS
They do help me
They release my emotions you see
They don't rhyme
all the time
and my spelling is intertwined
but it helps
so I continue
your heart is within you
Healing your feelings
POEMS
They are relieving
RS

Making Sense of Time

A moment in time
A second would be fine
or a minute
or an hour
Just a moment...
I'll let you know how long that really is
I'll figure it out
RS 3-22-95

Face Trip

The question on this Valentine's day is;
What do I feel
What do I say
If love is the true picture
And the heart is in glory
Then what do I do now
Other than tell this story
My heart feels broken
My life is unspoken
Changes are in place
Tears on my face.
RS 2-8-95

Thinking a Fix

When we reminisce
About our former husband or wife
The images we see
Will make us wonder about our life
Was it so bad
Was it so good
Did we reach a level?
We promised we never would
Now here we are
Not sure about our feelings
Protecting ourselves
While our hearts are healing
RS 3-22-95

Please Don't Share

Disturbed
Perturbed
Mad, angry and hurt
Why did you tell me
The results of a flirt
Telling me personal details
Of your personal life
Does it count anymore
You're my X wife?!
Add a crack to my heart
A tear to my eye
Bad memories to my mind
Reestablish sadness
You are so kind
RS 3-15-95

Special Message from Above

Russ

Things happen in our lives that don't always add up in any particular way until several incidents start to mingle together in an abstract kind of way. Is there a special message being sent from above? Is it a training process for us to figure out what life is really all about? Is it all coincidental? It sure makes me think about how many times I have been lucky. I think I finally got some answers. I'll share after I tell you my stories.

I started out life like a normal kid. I was told about all the silly stuff I did from my parents, sisters, and brother. There were a couple of things that I can still remember that came very close to me losing my life. Somehow I managed to survive. At about two years old, I drank lighter fluid – more than enough to kill me. My parents just happened to catch me soon enough and be close enough to the hospital to save me. I can only imagine what that tasted like, and that was just the start.

I swam all the time when we lived in Oahu, Hawaii. I made the swim team when I was three with the six-and-under division. I could swim up and back in the freestyle before anyone else could reach one end. Swimming was part of my life so I was never afraid. My family would go to the beach all the time. Our parents and neighbors watched us.

On a normal day, the current would have a particular direction or maybe two. On that day, it pulled out from the shore, probably half of a mile. I could feel myself being pulled away from the shoreline. The people on the beach got smaller and smaller. I learned enough not to fight against the flow, but I could still feel it pulling me further out. I don't know why I really never got scared. I was very lucky. After about twenty minutes, the current started to move me back closer to the shore. I swam as hard as I could to get back to the beach.

I remember walking back to our car to tell my family what had happened. I was so tired that I guess I didn't make my point about what had really taken place. Or perhaps I held back so my parents wouldn't say I couldn't swim alone anymore. As I write this, I can see myself in the ocean. It actually scares me and makes me look above.

I lived in Colorado Springs, Colorado for eighth through eleventh grades, in the early 70s. During that time, the Garden of the Gods Park was easy to climb. Several shanks of huge rock at a vertical angle stuck hundreds of feet straight up. There are mad stories about how they got their name. The sun always seemed to break through the clouds and make them shine all the time.

I began to climb the mountains one day, thinking it was fairly easy and safe. I worked my way up a section toward the back where no one was. I reached an area about six stories high, where the two slabs started to split apart. The rock was fairly sandy and slippery as I got higher. At that moment, I realized I was in a very scary position. I had stepped from one side to the other, and I was stuck. I couldn't see any place to step up or down. I think I simply said, "Oh shit."

It is hard to explain what happened next. I had to find a way to get down. Then, all of a sudden, I looked across to the other side and thought I saw a place to step and another place to grab. So I went for it. As I reached over and stepped all the way across, I got my balance. I moved to the side and stepped down a couple feet to get secure.

I looked back at the places I had stepped, and they were just gone. There is no way I should have made it over. You may think I just didn't see where I had stepped, but I have no reason to make up stories. It has stuck in my head for over twenty years. I have told hundreds of people. I wish I could go back and find the spot. The Garden of the Gods is completely different now, and you can't hike that area anymore.

The next year, I really wanted a motorcycle. I didn't have the money to buy a new bike so I got a Honda 250hp – nothing really special, but it ran. My parents didn't know I had it, nor was I old enough to ride. One day, I went up into the mountains at the base of the Pikes Peak to ride around.

You have to picture the top with a mixture of mountains that have valleys in between. In one area, they taught people how to hang-glide because there are lots of sections that have the land drop-off to the base at various levels.

On that one day, when I was exploring on the top level of one section with the simple dirt street, the hang gliders were about 400 feet off to my left. It was fun to watch them fly. I should have paid more attention to the path I was on because it ended. Off I went. Flying down a thirty-plus grade, grabbing the front end, still in gear, bumping over rocks. My life was in my hands and feet. I was scared to death.

Somehow I made it to the base, even though I was moving pretty fast. As I started to slow down and think, "Thank God I made it," I realized a concrete trench was right in front of me. I crashed directly into the wall. I must have been out for a while, because when I looked up there were people above looking down.

The motorcycle was on my left leg, burning my skin. Part of the mirror was in my side. The people came down to help me. As they pulled the bike off and looked at all the blood, they kept saying, "We can't believe you're still alive." I was happy to be living, but very pissed I destroyed my bike.

Then I started to think about what had happened and how I survived. Why had I survived? I sure was lucky, again.

Now I had to hide from my parents so they couldn't see the scrapes all over my left leg and back. When I got home, I snuck into my room. I was really sore and tired. I hid my clothes, rinsed off my body, and went to bed. The next morning, I got up to go to school. I was half asleep when I went to take a shower. Just as I got into the water, I could hear my mom scream. She found blood all over the sheets. I had lost a ton of blood that night and had survived. Boy, did I get in trouble! That motorcycle was pretty much destroyed. I still wonder how I made it. Another reason to be really happy with my life.

My next adventure was at the Army post in Fort Huachuca. My father was a Brigadier General and the Commander of the Post when I was a senior in high school. The post was one hundred years old and right next to Sierra Vista, Arizona. You had to drive through different parts of the post to get to Sierra Vista. When you first left the barracks, there was a two-way lane for about a mile, then it split into a one-way lane that wrapped around the base of the hill toward the exit. You couldn't see around the corner, and it's a good sixty-degree turn.

One dark night, I had one of those fights with my girlfriend that really pissed me off. She accused me of doing something that made me jump into my car and drive like a crazy Mario Andretti. As I built up speed through the two-lane street, all of a sudden I saw the green eyes of a black deer in the middle of the road. I slammed the brakes and came to a streaking stop. The black deer just stared at me for a second, turned his head and walked into the dark. As my heart slowed down, I started to move forward again.

All of a sudden, a car came rushing around the corner the wrong way, careening at sixty mph. I was shocked. If I had kept going – if the deer hadn't stopped me – I would have had a head-on collision. I knew I was going over the speed limit. What if that black deer hadn't stopped me? Did it happen for a reason, or was it just luck? Why do I seem to have so many near-death experiences?

So life has moved on and I'm in my thirties now. What possibly could happen to me now? Well, it was an experience I'll never forget even though I can't remember anything.

3/20 – 103

Thoughts today had gone away...
but came back to me anyway...
RS 4-95 (Boy am I sad)

Two Ways to Grip

Here I sit as a Grip,
It's a good day
Yet nine years ago today
The grip I had
Was on my heart
RS- Working on commercial as a Grip

Erase

Please stop thinking
Please stop hurting
Make my heart stop beating
Turn off my memory
Release my emotions
Let me take control
RS 4-95

3/23 – 109

Statement: It's funny how life goes by
and your memory never does...
RS 4-95

Thought of the day
Don't go away
I really want to stay
I'm faithful & pleased
In my Former life
I was teased
Now I know Where
                    everything goes)
life, love & feelings
I can now stop & smell the Rose

B 8-5-95

Getting Better Every Day

Gee, we used to love
We used to cry
We did smile a lot
Together
It's been so hard

Day After

So I am sore today
Inside and out
I've learned so much
I'm ready to play
RS 4-95

Punt That Away

Working out to kill the pain
Hurts so good
Am I sane
Sometimes feelings need to be released
Lifting weights
Sweating
Can pain be deceased
Time goes by
My body is better
Bigger, stronger
Ready to be tempted
RS 4-1-95

Forget To Remember

You could say
I'm at that part of my life
That I don't miss my Ex-wife
But then again
You could say
She will never ever get away
RS 4-4-95

Another World

In the shutter of my mind
Opening and closing
All the time
Thought pattern changing
rearranging
exchanging
Healing and squealing
There is no pattern
I'm not on Saturn
RS 4-6-95

Please Get Better

Always say
As time goes by
That our memories... should fly away
... they should melt
... they should stop
... they should change
But how do you alternate your memory?
When time has passed
Results are the same
And your feelings are still there
Just buried in your mind
Still melting your heart
RS 4-24-95

Bad Shit

Here I am on the pot today
Telling my emotions to go away
Do I try to extract and remove?
But I guess my brain is not in the groove
AH... then the pattern is released
Better, although it will never cease
RS 4-24-95

Building Up To Fall

I was thinking of a poem
When I was on my way back home
And boy did it rhyme
It was right on time
Building, getting better
Close to the words – I could almost remember
Then it all came back
Wow, what a rhythm and beat
Then I realized what it was saying
And it crashed me back on my feet
RS 4-95

Whose Memorial?

Here it is Memorial Day
Shall I pray or should I play
Watch TV
Reminisce
Read the articles
Search for a kiss
My feelings wonder
Choices fly
I guess I can simplify
... and then begin to cry
RS 5-29-95

Late At Night

Feelings, semi-controlling
Brain, adjustment critical
Your past, cruises by
Control, makes you cry
Time, up then down
Distance, semi-reachable
Pets, love reminders
RS 4-25-95

I Reminisce Too Much

Although I am coming back
And I guess I did have a life before you
It was really great
Well, now I know
AFTER is even better
RS 4-28-95

Zap!

A seizure
Is a brain squeeze
A nerve teaser
Memory erased
Reality encased
Everything is out of place
RS 5-30-95 (Had mini-seizure)

46

Seize Me

Russ

A seizure is different for everyone, but it is basically a power overflow in your brain. There can be a sign of some kind that lets you know something is wrong, like ringing in your ears or feeling like you have been surrounded by solid glass. You can see, but you can't hear. If I got worse, I would lose the ability to think or remember.

A word faded into my thought patterns and floated round and round in my mind. For me, it was something related to the cancer, everything that I have thought about my experience – cancer, tumor, surgery, dilation, narration, seizure, medicine, hospital, recovery, damage, pain, suffering, nurses, doctor, chemotherapy, surgery room, MRI, stretcher, ambulance, medic, oxygen mask. Round and round my mind went.

It hurts your head. It scares you. It takes over. You build up tension and pain. Your ears ring louder and louder. It's a deep, uncomfortable feeling in your ears and head. You feel like you've lost your breath. You feel like you're sick to your stomach.

The pain and confusion took me to the most uncomfortable places.

It finally hits this maximum level that literally shuts off the power switch in your life. You are unconscious. It's like an escape from pain and suffering.

I can only look back, and that is how the thoughts come out of my memory.

I just had a mini-seizure two hours ago and I'm trying to describe what it is like to have a grand-mal seizure. I'm also fighting a pretty bad headache.

When I started to wake up, I was so confused. I usually don't know where I am or what has happened. There have been cases when I opened my eyes and had emergency personnel all around me. There was a lead person who was trying to wake me up. He asked me questions like, "What is your name? Do you know what day it is? What time it is? Where are you?"

I tried to speak, but the words would not come out of my mouth. I felt like a baby. I couldn't talk, but inside my mind I was frustrated that the right words wouldn't come out. It could take five to ten minutes before a real word would make its way out of my mouth. I slurred and said "shit" every time I messed up my statement. I started to understand what had happened.

It's like beginning to see a picture you have seen before. I felt like I knew what it was. But inside I was staring at the face that was there and nothing became clear. I scrunched my eyes and tried to understand what happened, but it was still not clear.

There is a rule with the ambulance companies. If the person that has been injured cannot respond properly within fifteen minutes, they have to take you to the emergency room. I learned that over time since I had taken several rides to the emergency room. I always got my memory back along the way.

It was never fun to realize what had just taken place. My wake up was extremely aggravating. I was inside the ambulance, strapped down on a stretcher, with an oxygen mask on my nose and mouth and some kind of medicine jammed into my vein. This was not very much fun to accept. Sirens blaring overhead and the medic sitting next to me checking my blood pressure, looking in my eyes, talking to me and getting all the pertinent information. I felt embarrassed, sad, and had a really bad headache.

As I arrived at the hospital, the next adventure would begin. I was transported into the E.R. and placed into my netted cubicle. The nurse would come in asking about who she should call, my insurance info, and all the details about my life. I got so frustrated. Waiting to see the doctor seemed to take forever. By that time, I was pretty much better. I learned it was best to have all the basic information related to my cancer in my possession.

Hurting Better

Here's my poem of the day
I'm confused and it won't go away
Pressure and stress
Bills and more bills
Doctors and pills
I'm going over the hills
Adapt and regress
Slow down in this mess
Patience and time
I will be fine
RS 5-30-95

Simple Note

Recovering is like hovering
We don't go up or down
There is just an occasional rise and fall
Life moves on... that is all
RS 6-95

Fire

Stars do sprinkle
They attract my view
Make me wonder
Where are you
Thinking and wondering
Exploring my thoughts
Did I learn
Or emotionally burn
On my flight
Of no concern
RS 6-95

On a Friday Night June 2, 1995

A moment in time
Days and nights rushed by
They reach their prime
Blend and defend
Answers to questions evolve
Questions to answers dissolve
Life moves on
RS

The Sport of Thinking

I dribble in my thoughts
I'm ready to shoot
The shot is blocked PERSONAL FOUL!
RS 6-95

Look Away

Look at the past and compare your life to today
Then forget yesterday and run away
Erase the negative slowly
Don't reminisce about the good things
They draw you back and spit you out
RS 6-2-95

Looking For What

Did you ever just sit there
With no particular thought on your mind
Staring out through the structures
Seeing, but feeling blind
Time moves on
Life continues
What is it you hope to find
RS 6-5-95

3/44 – 158

Trying to make decisions, then missing holding hands
Life is short, so they say
I still enjoy it, every day
Although there are always times
When I reminisce
I miss your presence
I crave your kiss
Life goes on and on
Feeling better in every way
I just need to tell my memory
To go far, far away

Breaking Out Of Here

Former wives
Still within our lives
Ask the favor
Request for held
Receive free assistance
Then lock the door
and free the slave
RS 6-19-95

Keep Standing

There is always a question within my mind
Was it love that I did find
Or was it just part of growing up
A test on my heart
A quiz on my emotions
Did I graduate with my divorce?
Or did I flunk and now have to go back to school
RS 6-19-95

Broken

My feelings tonight are
A strange mixture of love and hate
In a changeable fixture
Adjustable – Combustible
Releasable – Incredible
Then, BOOM – Out Of Order
RS 6-19-95

There was one day
we did march

Step by step
our hearts did part
our lives did
      change
The future was
            strange
The past in our min
Did rearrange

3/28/95

I Fight and Try to Adjust

I can't, then I can
Then it starts all over again
Erase the emotions
Protect the heart
Control the feelings
Work around yourself
Clear your memories
Adjust that dial
The story you are about to hear is true
Her name was changed
... to protect the innocent
RS 6-19-95

Black/White

Life can be so funny
Is it love or faith or money
We seem to change
Then rearrange
Is it dark or is it sunny
RS 6-22-95

3/35 – 136

Reactions sometimes surprises
They can bring tears to your eyes
Then again even though they are negative
Somehow becomes a sedative
RS 6-22-95

Good Time

What a week
What a day
Hey, I'm OK
YEA!
RS 6-26-95

Check The rules

Commitment in a relationship
Who wins?
What about practice
And is there a coach
Where is the best place to play?
Is there ever a winner
Better ask the ref!
RS 6-26-95

Formula

I value my life - Thank God
I regret my X wife – that's odd
The two mixed together make sod*
*One grows – the other is dirt
RS 6-26-95

Lovefurr

My cat in my lap
His eyes green and fur black
The love in his heart
Helps my life grow back
RS 6-26-95

I'm Crying In The Sun

Sometimes I have a ball
Just walking in the mall
You know I do love it all
Although my X can make my heart stall
RS 6-26-95

Cleat It Up!

Life in the mood to rhyme this time
Feeling pretty good, actually fine
Can't ask for much more –
Well... except help removing all this slime
RS 6-26-95

Think Back

I reminisce about love
Relationships – you need special gloves
Go out on the streets and look
Slowly search, but watch out for that hook
Think and wonder, the best way to wander
RS

Hiding The Clock

Why do I try to escape?
Hide with a smile behind a cape
Make all those around me
Think I am doing fine
When I really am not happy
I seem to be counting my time
RS 7-95

Closed Door

I do have spirit
Can't always hear it
I perilously cheer it on
It's like writing a song
A shield to protect
Control of my soul
RS 7-95

3/10 – 68

Some things are slow
Like rebuilding in the snow
Love must be a show
Waiting for my heart to grow
Healing takes a lot of time you know...
RS 7-95

Hiding In The Breeze

It's a cool summer night
Perky clouds drift in the breeze
Good feelings surround me
Slashing and dashing in the trees
Deep in my heart confusion abides
Still lonely and protecting
That's why my heart still hides
RS 7-95

Counting

Reality is so hard
Convince yourself it will all work
Deny the down and the doom
Will anything happen
Very late or very soon?
RS

True

Invariable is terrible
X 10
RS

Forgetter

All the decisions we have to make
Look into the future
But not too far, for heaven's sake
Convince yourself to just live for the day
Still make plans
... for your memories to go away
RS 7-95

Oops... Trip

So often I find myself
Trying to control my mind
Looking into my brain
And what do I find
Different images and patterns
Thoughts to protect and deny
But I always seem to stumble
Then trip over... Why?
RS

The Blues

I want to erase my memory
My past love won't leave my mind
The loss of my thoughts would be so kind
Too many reminders linger
I am becoming a Blues singer
RS 7-16-95

Sigh n' Cry

A flash in the sky
A tear in my eye
Bad feelings make me cry
Lack of passion makes me sigh
RS 7-16-95

Open Your Life

Lights – Camera – Action
Interlude with passion
Don't direct to control
Let things go as a roll
The theme will slide
Go up and down then glide
Explore yourself don't hide
RS 7-16-95

Dr. Quack

Thought pattern out of whack
Thinking too much
You'll need a quack
Feelings are uncomfortable
Decisions diabolical
Memory control next to impossible
RS 7-22-95

Don't Remind Me

To view other lovers
Try to extract their feelings
It has some ups and downs
As your emotions start reeling
Another perspective and remission
Reminds you of your loveless condition
RS 7-22-95

Learn Now

Kids, there's a story
Some people glow with their glory
Others seem to put up with their stress
Those without dreams become depressed
RS 7-22-95

Mix Each Other Up

Far away from normal life
Single, lonely without a wife
Married men say you are lucky
They wish they were single too
Questions in your mind
You don't know what to do
RS 7-22-95

Now That's a Good Game

I played great tonight
I won the game to my delight
Sometimes you have to give it your all
Push it to your limit, have a ball
Never give up
Never stop trying
Get over your mistakes
Get over your crying
Life is really so good
Enjoy every moment you see
Sometime have fun just like you were three
When you think about the end
It shall come to all of us someday
So just enjoy your life and play, play, play
RS 7-22-95

Going the Other Way

Well, the comics usually are funny
Sometimes you laugh and they cheer you up
But today I read them, they were only OK
Then one was a reminder, sad you could say
It drew out thoughts of how things have changed
How ONE life went the other way and rearranged
Who is to blame... who is searching for fame
Believe me, nothing in life will ever be the same
RS 7-30-95

Let It Go!

Tonight I can't seem to stop
I am moving my feelings
From the bottom to the top
All I see and feel is real
My future is a special deal
I can't seem to predict
I don't want to be sick
Let it out, write it, release it
Damn - I'm trying
But I can't replace it
RS 7-30-95

Pain

Thinkin', thinkin', about my wife
Draws emotions – causes strife
To think too much about the past
Is really a painful PAIN IN DA ASS!
RS 7-30-95

Good Past For All

I was in the church the other day
I picked up the Bible
and my mind did say
How could this be written
In any old way?
It could not be a line
or maybe up in a day
Even in many, many years
in this particular display
I thought and I thought
and suddenly said, HEY!
This is really all truthful
now I'm OK
RS 1995
Written while on break from World Gym at Faith Lutheran
Church '95

3/11 – 72

When feelings come out in ink
You think and hope these thoughts don't stink
But Hey, I am trying not to sink
RS 1995

3/7 – 59

Still in good shape
Working out
Pumping up
As the body gets better
Tell my memory to SHUT UP!!!

Note

Being alone is not always what you would not
understand
By yourself you can enjoy your own life, the way you
want to.
Adjusting is not always the way you really think
or understand
RS

Rhyming Thoughts

Are here today
Sometimes I want them
to go away...
RS 8-95

Hang Up and Heal

When I'm feeling all alone
I thank God I have a phone
I can talk, cry and laugh and sing
But I can always hang up
To heal and hear my life "sting"
RS 8-95

3/39 – 145

OK, I'm in semi-endless happiness
Even though I occasionally miss your kiss
Life is still getting better like this
RS 8-1-95

Up Then Doom

Having brunch in a wonderful city
People here are so nice and pretty
Viewing the mountain
The middle of town
Then I realize I'm all alone and really go down
RS 8-5-95

4-24-95

We always say
   as time goes by
that our memories
      should fly away
....they should melt
.... they should stop
....they should change
But how do you alternate
      your memory?
when time has passed
results are the same
and your feelings are still there
just burried in your mind
   and still melting your heart

B

Change My Future

There was one day
We did march
Step by step
Our hearts did part
Our lives did change
The future was strange
The past in our minds
Had to rearrange
RS 3-28-95

Smell The Roses

Thought of the day
Don't go away
I really want to stay
I'm faithful and pleased
In my former life
I know I was teased
Now I know where everything goes
Life, Love and feelings
I can now stop and smell the roses
RS 8-5-95

Fly In The Sky
Religion is like a pigeon
There are many different kinds
They all can fly
up to the sky
Some follow smoothly
others cruise
Then many follow a pattern
a schedule, then snooze
But no matter how you view the flight
What you believe in
will help you win the fight
RS 8-5-95

Court Fighting
Desperation and perpetuation
Oh this is such a wonderful Nation
Sometimes causing total frustration
Fighting court is humiliation
RS 9-1-95 (Going to court fighting a ticket)

Sealed Tight
A horde of hate
How is it handled?
A crack in your heart
How do you deal with it?
And what about your overall feelings
Why are they sealed?

Need Repair

Waiting for the phone to ring
Waiting for the birds to sing
Wondering what my thoughts will bring
Fighting that memory sting
RS 11-13-95

Document

Good days
Bad days
My mind in a purple haze
Fighting and resting
Studying and testing
As my life moves on, I am attesting
RS 11-13-95

Release Me

Releasing my thoughts on paper
Feeling the words as I write
My pen moves on
My mind starts a journey
There is no compliance
There is no scrutiny
RS 11-13-95

How Do I Block?

Variety is the spice of life
Not necessarily the husband and wife
But interference causes strife
How we plan
How we decide
There are some feelings
We cannot hide
RS 12/9

Oh Yes! Oh No!

Days are up
Nights are down
Feelings always go round and round
No balance
No synchrony
Battle for your life
Hold on... Let Go
12/95

Lost

There are times, days, future and past
We think so much, Will it last?
Do we use our minds way too much?
Is there a balance
Is there an answer
Was my notification my cancer
Or that roaming, searching wild panther
RS 12/95

Emotional Moments

It's part of our life
All those questions in the air
There are no easy answers
For a husband and wife
There are no easy questions
Or it would not be so emotional
RS 12-20-95

Dial That Channel

I am weary now
Tired in many ways
3/45- 160

4-25

Its Funny how life goes by
and your memorys never does
~~flash prints~~

Feelings, semi-controlling
Brainy, Ajstment critical
your past, wizzes bye
Control, makes you cry
Time, up, then down
Distance, semi-Reachable
Pets, Love reminders

4-25
Late at
night -
afterpractice

Making Spirits Bright

Louisa ~ December 1995

I met Russ at a Christmas party at my house in 1995. I can distinctly remember turning my head and being struck by his imposing size and inescapable aura. Tall with broad shoulders, his 6'6" frame overshadowed my own 6'stature. With his long, dark hair and piercing blue eyes, Russ looked like an amazing cross between Tom Selleck and Yanni. He was the most handsome man in the room.

There was an energetic exchange between us – not sexual, though. Not exactly what the French would call a coup de foundre, "love at first sight," but more like warm goosebumps all over my body where each hair rose up to notice.

We soon found that we worked in the same industry – video and TV production. I was embarking on a new television project and he listened intently with a deep presence, offering to connect me with key people.

I felt uncomfortable with his deep gaze. It was as if he could see into my soul – something that I didn't truly understand and yet instinctively knew I was ready for. I'd pause and talk to another guest and when I turned around, there he was seeking more.

He asked me out. On our first date, he let me know that he was three years past his "death date," and was in, as he described it, "limbo land." He was in remission from a brain tumor. He was also recently divorced. He was alive and unsure of his purpose. He was tentative about dating and got into details about his cancer. If he was trying to scare me away, it worked.

1/10 – 28

SEQUENCE OF EVENTS;
BORN
RAISED
LOVE
DAZED
RECOVERY
HAZED
LIVING
GIVING
PRAISING
RAISING
RISING
RS 1/96

1/11 – 29

How does one avoid time?
Why does pain slow down the clock?
Questions with no answers
Feelings with no control
Can we make adjustments
Can we level out
Hit cruise control
Be ready for landing...
RS 1/96

In the shutter of my mind
Opening & closing
all the time
Thought patterns changing
  rearranging
  exchanging
Healing & squeewelling

There is no patterns
It's not on Saturn.

RB 4/6/95

Accept It

HERE I am in a place in space
Trying to keep up with my pace
Accept all the circumstances
Thank God for your chances
Remember those dances
Feel positive trances
RS 1/96

Celebrate

Celebrate, celebrate
dance to the music
you have your life
you have no wife
go out and use it without any strife
RS 1/96 (Louisa)

1/18 – 22

Too many thoughts are confusing
Memories are abusing
Changes are solutions
But sometimes are contusions
RS 1/96

Equals?

GET A GRIP = TAKE A TRIP
TRIP AND FALL= HAVE A BALL
TAKE A CHANCE = SEARCH FOR ROMANCE

1/7 – 20

Waiting, Waiting
interrogating
Thoughts travel too much
Questions avoid answers as such
Positive aura - life is so good
Decisions, Decisions
Solutions, Oh I wish I could find them
RS 1/96

Saturn

Leery thoughts of memory
Erase, change, be cheery
Make up your thinking pattern
My next stop will be Saturn
RS 1/12/96

Magic Island

So much luck
So many good things
What a positive attitude I have now
As the Pirate sings
"Har me matty How Ya be"
"Jump off the ship on the count of three"
I guess I could swim, far, far away
Find that magic island in my mind today
RS 1/12/96 (Day after Fox offered me a contract)

1/11 – 30

THINKING, THINKING
Is this the beginning of life
Or the beginning of strife
So much to do
So much to change
I guess I must rearrange
RS 1/12/96

_____ ION

If I can release my tension
On this particular dimension
Then I still need a session
Concerning my regression
For LOVE is an obsession
RS

Why Did I Get Sick

Here it is the poem of the day
As I sit all alone
On a sunny, sunny day
Wondering and thinking
No particular thoughts
I still feel so lucky
What was I taught...?
RS May 11, 1996

Crash

Moments in time flush through our minds
Distributing feelings of all kinds
There is no particular reason
Nor is there a specific season
As we think about the past
Our minds break just like delicate glass
RS May 12, 1996

Mother's Day

Russ

It was a Sunday afternoon and my mom and dad had come to spend some time with me. It had been nine months since my surgery and I was still not at full speed. We were watching football, which is a favorite thing we shared. I got up to get something out of the bedroom. As I came down the hallway, I looked out the front door and saw my mother standing outside, looking into the distance. I walked outside and asked her how she was.

She turned toward me with an expression on her face I'd never seen. An emotional combination of love and compassion overwhelmed me. She looked me square in the eyes and grabbed my shoulders strongly and said, "Don't you die before I do! Don't you leave before I do. Do you understand what I mean? Do you understand?"

Flabbergasted by the look on her face, I knew what she was feeling. I looked straight back into her eyes and said, "I promise you, Mom. I promise." She looked closely into my eyes to make sure I had understood what she meant. Believe me, I can still see her face as I write this. I could feel the depth of her emotions and love. When I talk to her, every so often, she will remind me of the promise that I made and that I never plan to break.

Mother's Day

Mother's Day is here to stay
We are so lucky, I'd like to say
As children we never knew
How much work Mom had to do
So take this time to tell your Mother
You Love Her more than any other
RS 1996 (Mothers Day- She just left after breakfast)

Divorce

And here is a signal to my "X"
I can write and think, are you perplexed
I don't think so
Because you really never did care
Not about anyone else
Just the style of your hair
RS May 12, 1996

Cats

I sit with my family of cats
It's a very warm Sunday so I'm wearing a hat
I don't know where my thoughts are at
Somehow this moment in time has placed me here
There have been forces that have been so severe
So I write this down to release
I do want my thoughts to be deceased
RS (Just out of nowhere)

Pump It Up

Here I sit at my desk again
My eyes are closed
My thoughts begin
What should I do today
How can I get away?
Decisions are frustrating they say
Try to turn up the volume
Get more power
Feel good feelings hour after hour
RS 5/13/96

Wondering

Sometimes I wonder about everything
I watch TV, read and sing
I'm still not sure what's best for me
Just now I think about climbing a tree
Get half way up
Grab a rope
Swing far, far away
Land on a steep slope
RS 5/13/96

Gym Poem

Here is my initial thought of the day
You can get up there in any old way
All you need is the spirit of life
Positive thought
And an image of the bright light
Never ever give up
And don't let go
But, be ready when its time
Because you shall know
RS (Taking break from World Gym at Church. This was when I started my first job after surgery to help myself get back into life. The gym was the level I had to begin with.)

Butt Poem

WHY is the question of the day?
There is no answer BUTT that's OK
RS (That means "a pain in the Butt")

Made It This Far

Here I lie in bed on a rainy cool night
Contemplating my life, so much out of sight
Wondering about my future, thinking about my fight
Well, what the heck, I've made it this far – to my delight
RS 7-96

3/8 – 62

I am not afraid, but I am sad
I don't think dying is that bad
It's the process
It's the changes
All the rearranges
Dealing with emotions
Adjusting to reality
I guess we all have to know
We will all be a fatality
RS 7-96

Strange Thoughts

If a fish is viscous
And also delicious
Is his life suspicious?
If a fish is rather hasty
And also very tasty
Do we chase or give space?
RS 7-96 (Just a strange thought about life...)

2/1 – 35

How do we decide what to do?
When there is no answer
If it is half one way
And two quarters the other
One has to look deep inside
Weigh it all out
It's OK if you still don't know
Which way to go
Or which way to stay
RS 7-23-96

Thinking About Death

It's creeping in
Slowly, but surely
Reality, step by step
Who do I talk to
What do I say
Deep down inside
Leaving is now OK
But it's when and how
Then I'm up, then down
How do I tell anyone
Then understand their response
Will it make me feel better
Could anything make a difference
Would it make me want to dance
Maybe I should go into a trance
RS 7-23-96

2/2 – 37

Wondering is like deliberating
We don't know where we are going
We are not sure when we will leave
We are basically lost and not convinced
Heading in the right direction
Did we make the right selection
RS 7-29-96 (At Steven's house in Colorado)

What Future?

How do I feel near the END?
Should I not think about it
Should I stand up shout about it
Hold it in and deliberate
Worry. Be scared. Contemplate.
Where is the answer
How do I adjust
Planning for the future
Is only a bust
RS 7-29-96

Questions???

Are there times in our lives?
When everything is tested
Our feelings on all sides
At this time the bad ones are protested
Is it a quiz from far above
A report due today about LOVE
How long do I have
What should I do right now
I am not really sure
And I don't know how
RS 7-30-96

Very Complicated

Ups and downs – all around
Recover, hover, wonder
No answers, more questions
Positive feelings - after negative
Moments of fear, stress and fatigue
Turnarounds, curves, elevation
A very, very complicated situation
RS 7-30-96

Tomorrow's Soon Enough

When feelings are obliterated
And balance is questionable
Tighten your defense system
Gear up, get your weapons ready
Hold yourself steady
Stock protection, be safe, keep your position
There shall always be a battle in life
Make the most of today
Tomorrow will be there soon enough
RS 7-31-96

Give Me Time

Please let me keep my vision
So I can lose my view of life
It would be like forgetting my religion
I promise to do those good things with no decision
You see I'm here to help everyone
I know I can, you know as well
With my eyes I'm so much better
Give me some time – I guarantee you can tell
RS 8-96

Accepting Death

Thank the Lord for the Life I have lived
For every day
For every night
And how ever many more I might
I have no fear of death now
I look forward to my rise
Happiness and love are in my eyes
Each moment is so wonderful now
I came so close to visit you.
When you are ready, I am too
RS (At church some Sunday '96)

3/1 – 46

Anticipation of your journey
Arrival to your goal
Enjoyment during those moments
Departure steals your soul
Remembering creates a spark
Forgetting makes life dark
RS 8-2-96

3/2 – 47

Paper and pen help me release sorrow
Power in my mind is my bow and arrow
Feelings going up, down, in and out
Moments of madness make me shout
Family and friends put that smile back on my face
Emotions now back and forth without a trace
RS 8-2-96

1/12 – 32

There are things that happen in the night
Dreams and sleep to our delight
Body and minds relax and lay straight
Thoughts about the future and their way out
Good feelings about life for today
Put a smile on my face – what more can I say
RS 8-3-96

Don't Grade Me

I do know how lucky I am
I realize life is a lot of work
It's OK to be on a journey with no map
All your feelings are like a test
There is no time period
There are no grades
There is no special answer
You have to keep trying
We know the story ends by dying
RS 8-2-96

Waiting To Work

Where did killing time begin
Counting each moment is no sin
Watching the clock go round and round
Listening to silence, diagnosing the sound
Wondering and waiting
Thinking about your life
Analyzing decisions you've made
Dealing with the past and the strife
As you "KILL" your time
And look back once again
You will regret not using every second
For the end may be rolling in
RS 8-10-96 (In Tucson, on video shoot waiting to work)

Embarking
Just feelin' good
Relaxed and real cool
I like everyday that I do live
It's what my head has to give
Let just easy thoughts embark
Don't try to conduct them from the start
Just let your karma trust 'um before you depart
RS

Screen Poem
As I write my thoughts onto the screen
I wonder where my mind has been
My fingers move
The letters display
There is no plan of attack
They just come out before I hit the sack
RS

Here, But I want to Go
Did you ever wonder why you are here
You're not too sure.
It's not too clear
Some people have to escape
Some just put in a tape
Others write or read stories that they dream about
We are here. Is there a way out?
RS (Note: I wanted to die)

Audios?

The day has come now when I must decide
Should I do this or that, hovers in my mind
As I think and wonder and express my thoughts
I confuse myself, should I or not…
RS

Auto Smile

Feeling better happens suddenly
Out of the blue
Before you know it
Smiling is retained for no reason
Good Karma
An accomplishment you have wanted
A chance you have been waiting for
The first time you didn't try to smile
Happiness came on auto
YES! Now you can move on
Thank you for the changes in my life
RS 10-9-96

Keep Life Stable

The end of the day and the night
Many hours have been a fright
In return money shall be received
Checks seem to leave us relieved
Society makes income important
Realism try to make you change
Deep inside we are animals
We live upon an earth we need to salvage
No matter how we live we are together
The things we do to our planet will last forever
RS 11-96

When a Friend Dies

There are so many stages in my life
I lost a friend
I lost my wife
Is it an emotional test from far above
Testing my feelings
Questioning my love
Situations beyond my control
People drifting
Losing their soul
I know we all must move on
I realize why people write a sad song
WHY? is asked all the time
There is no answer
There is no rhyme
RS 11-18-96 (Services for a friend tonight)

Power Down

When people leave without saying good-bye
Then they never return, of course we cry
We wonder...
We ask all those questions;
Why? and Why? and Why?
Resolve those feelings somehow
Think and cry throughout that moment
In your life, no, you can't make a plan
We all must just live on and on
It's still not easy, no one said it would be
To live on, up, down and over
That's the pattern we must deal with
So, here we go folks
Get ready to take off and make a crash
RS 11-18-96

Goodbye, Farewell

Life and death don't play with each other
There's just that Thought from beginning to end
I guess when we least expect it, it happens
That rolling round and round, up and down – CRASH
Possession is verified. Action begins and ends
Stories start. Memories flow. Experiences renewed
Feelings, now there's a tidal wave... SPLASH!
Thinking about reality. Fatality. Escape
Spectrum of lives, people, months and years
Sorrow. Sadness. Realization. Frustration
Goodbye, farewell – Thank You. God Bless
RS 11-18-96 (After Tony C funeral)

Bump Into

Meeting out in the blue
Memories and feelings just flew
Thoughts incised my soul
Blood flow increased throughout
Good feelings empowered my mind
Eye to eye
Face to face
Silence
Love, power built passion
Reality ended
RS 12-2-96

Can't Figure It

Lights are all about
Do they mean we know why?
Many thoughts are passed around
From the sky to the ground
All kinds of feelings abound
Cards and presents
Ads and sales
Colors and lights
Special events
All these things move on and on
Your ears keep ringing
Songs dominate the sun
Thoughts deep down inside
Feelings bounce around and digress
Is your life the way you want it
Or are all changes a stress
RS 12-7-96

Long Confused Thought

If all of your feelings are within
When does release begin
How do we know what they are
The good ones, the bad ones
All those sad ones
Confuses in between
Will time change the pattern
Do we learn as we go along
and then change our feelings completely
When we hear a song
So why do I write all this
To explain to myself my brain pattern
It is OK to fluctuate
TO go on and on
to wonder and wonder
then wander and wander
Please help me find an answer
I need to control my soul
... OK, I feel a little better now
RS 1-13-97

Irony

The thought of the moment concerned me
I was not sure what it was that I was feeling
I was not entertained
I was not uncomfortable
But I still could not adjust
Was it the long ago life
Could it be a step that I missed
Was it that girl that I met
and remembering our first kiss
Thinking as I write this on paper confusion continues
I miss someone
I wish things could be different
Now I have to move on
Still no complaints about life
Maybe that's the part that's so hard
RS 1-13-97

Emotional Pain

After conversations with friends
I discovered that there are always ends
Partings, distance, removal
Changes that will never get approval
Pain throughout the body, mind and soul
Life without memories and a giant black hole
We need to resolve, solve, find a solution
Feelings are ruined – emotional pollution
RS 3-3-97 (Friends moving)

2/4 – 40

So many sides
Various slides
Creations
Distraction
Opposite directions
Too many decisions to be made
In the dark
Not in the shade
RS 3-3-97

2/4 – 41

To think too much about all that is around you
Creates a structure that can't be controlled
Positive feelings are released to help
You give so much from your heart and soul
Hoping and praying
Thinking about all you've been saying
Feeling guilty in some ways
You feel good and then you're down
Wishing everyone could be enjoying their lives
From the sky to the ground
RS 3-3-97

All the decisions we have
 to make
Looks into the future
 But not too far
 for heaven sake
Convince yourself to just
 live for the day
Still make plans
 for your memory to go away

7-30-95

So often I find myself
 trying to control my mind
looking into my brain
 and what do I find
Different images & patterns
thoughts to protect and deny
But I always seem to stumble
 and trip over why?

Way

Changes, changes, rearranges
Decisions, decisions, under conditions
Thoughts = confusion = dilution
This way, that way – any way, every way
Best way?
RS 3-5-97 (Full-time job offered... Great Scott!!)

2/5 – 43

Solve and resolve
Feel better all over
Satisfy you former feelings
Luck is a glory of sorts
Relief from sadness and madness
Life moves on any way it glows
Every way it goes
Decisions have an effect
Movement continues
Let your soul roll
RS 3-7-97

2/5 – 44

What did my mind ask my soul
I have no clue at all
I don't have to ask
I can't tell
I can't say
Make all of this go away
Is it all still here with no changes to be?
No, because now we can't see

Pondering

So here I sit on a moonlight night
My mind is pondering and wondering
Decisions to be made are before me
Directions to proceed are beyond
Thinking of what may be
How can I see - how can I tell
One direction may be the best
Yet the other may be a test
To wait for the moment is obscure
Hoping it will be the right one
...Well, you can tell I'm not sure
RS 3-21-97 (Offered to work on IMPACT show)

Fighting Hurts All

The last conversation I had tonight
Began a process of suicidal fright
I could feel a "give up" on each end was in process
There is no way it can be stopped
People all around will lose the battle
The riders want to jump off the saddle
Ride away to another place in their time
Letting go
No more enjoying
Suffering to the end
What a loss
RS 6-30-97

Scriptures

On the way to home today scriptures came to mind
Many different images appeared everywhere
Some were strange, some were kind
Relic movements abounded
The past revolved
Changes in ranges beyond consideration
Grown – re-growth taking place
Structure abounding on newness in this lifetime
RS 12-97

Trying To Forget

Contemplating the future ahead
Thinking about all the changes
Regretting some decisions
Rejoicing over others
Things of all kinds stroll in and out
Memories, thoughts, emotions divide
Life that we live is on no specific pattern
Dealing with everyone and everything
Which is the right way to go
How does one accept reality
We plan for the future and live for the day
Try to forget yesterday
RS

Slightly Brittle

I'm still here
What a turn around
From the bottom to the middle
I'm slightly brittle
Changes are normal
Dealing with them is a test
Steady as she goes
The future no one knows
RS 7-31-96

4/1 – 179

Out of Nowhere… Just on computer (JOC)
Insight to describe all the mental activity taking place
Descriptions are blending disorder within my face
Deceptions rush out from deep inside
There seems to be a moment that I must decide
Action abounds and astounds
Questionnaire alignments rearrange
Moments of discretion, possession and arising
Now the moment fluctuates back to center
I am inspired again to approach and tempt her
RS 7-28-97

Yoga Class Then Dinner

A wonderful time together
in beautiful Summer weather
There is very little that can be asked for all together
When your heart beats
When you can't stop smiling
You can't ask for anything more
Life sure can make changes
in your mind, body and soul
Without any product what-so-ever, your life is whole
RS 7-30-97

HELP... I Need Somebody

Awareness of life and love comes out of nowhere
Thoughts assist you to decide strategy
Other people in your life can change you
and increase your structure
Living in this world is really very simple in every way
We all ask for too many answers to questions
When we already know answers
Take your life into your own heart
You can accomplish anything you need
RS 8-16-97

Oh Just Seize Me

Another moment of life
Certain things happen to revive my strife
There are changes of all different kinds
Adjustment is converting my mind
Dealing with all that happens to you
Is so damn difficult when you're never through
RS 10-23-97 (Having mini-seizures – four to forty per day)

Special Agent Man

Here I am writing about the end
Thinking about all the things I want to send
Trying to put feelings on paper
It's a specialized special agent caper
Can I get everything in the proper order
Will I say enough or too much.
Is there a specified form with a specific border
I'm just trying to pass along my thoughts
Share my feelings
Spread my love
Make everyone happy
Just like the man above
RS 8-1-96

Word Has It

Louisa 1998

In 1998, I heard through our mutual grapevine that Russ was going to have another surgery. He could lose his sight, or even his ability to speak. I called him, full of worry and trepidation. But as usual, he put me at ease with his confidence and positive attitude. I stumbled over my words as we ended our call, trying so hard to hold my feelings for him inside and not wanting to let go of our virtual connection.

He had given me a photograph he had taken of a sunset. On the side, he wrote, "Love, Russ." I had that photo near my desk. It was a tangible reminder of him. When I hung up the phone, I said to it, "God, please either take Russ or give him a full remission."

6-5-95 ✗

Did you ever just sit there
 With no particular thought on your mind
Staring out thru the structure
 Seeing, but feeling blind
Time moves on
and life continues
 What is it you hope to find

I dribble in my thoughts
 I'm ready to shoot
The shot is blocked
 Personal Foul!

114

Be Careful

Russ

Here we go again... Yes, I could feel something change. It had been six years since my last brain surgery and I started to have mini-seizures every so often. Physically, I continued to rebuild my body. It had been two years since I had even had any seizures at all and I was feeling solid.

I had my MRI at Barrow Neurological Institute and met with Doctor Shapiro. As we did the normal tests with every visit – stand and spread my arms and touch my nose with my eyes closed – I knew I was flunking. I wasn't even close. Then we went to the look at the MRI and the change was evident. Cancer the size of my pinkie had grown inside the open cavity from the last surgery. It was pretty clear what was next.

I was scheduled for surgery on March 3, 1998. The same surgeon, Dr. Barranco, would operate, but there would be a few changes. My parents accompanied me to my pre-op visit. Dr. Barranco described how he would do the "clean up" as he put it. The good news: I would be unconscious the whole time. The bad news: I may lose my vision or the ability to speak.

Can you imagine losing your vision or speech after almost forty years? How would I adapt? Where would I go to learn? What would I do at a restaurant, shopping store, sports game, or anywhere for that matter? The tumor was so close to that part of my brain, but what were my choices? I just asked him to be careful and they all kind of smiled. I gave him a thumbs up signal and smiled back.

I was ready to check in and go through the patient process yet again. I guess when you know what is about to happen it is a lot easier to go through the motions. I don't like getting my name bracelet on. For some reason it makes me think about the negative side of surgery. Then again, I want them to give me the right kind of surgery. I don't think I'm pregnant, after all.

It's the same getting into your surgical pajamas with your butt shining out the back. It's normal and a little embarrassing. You kind of give up like a little kid and let them take over.

Now it's on to have surgery. The path seems clean, bright, and too short. I wish I didn't have to go. As we pass the waiting area, my parents, my girlfriend, and Pastor Staats come out to see me. It is hard to really talk. There is not very much to say. I know I will be unconscious. I am not going to worry. I trust everyone on the crew. I tell my parents I'll be fine, and feel their love and support. My girlfriend gives me a kiss and tells me she loves me. Pastor Staats and I talk about relaxing and believing in God. We say a strong prayer together that makes me feel calm and comfortable about whatever happens.

They rolled me through the huge automatic doors leading to the operating room. The same specialists were waiting for me. They had adapted the surgical table this time to fit my height. People worked all around me but no one looked at me directly or said anything. Dr. Barranco walked in and said hi, and reassured me about what was about to happen.

The needles were stuck into my veins in my hand and arms. As the specialist prepared the anesthesia I looked around the room, feeling cold and a little scared. I could taste the same gasoline smell and then the room began to swirl around. It's like when you are falling asleep in a dream after drinking too much alcohol. Everyone disappeared.

The next thing I remembered was getting sick to my stomach. I could see the high-tech equipment all around me. I felt high and confused. A nurse came over to me and said one thing to me but I'm not really sure what she asked. I tried to go back to sleep but she woke me up and asked my name. I felt really strange. I just kind of looked at her and tried to remember who I was. Then it started to come back to me. I said my name out loud and she smiled. I didn't realize how lucky I was still be able to talk. I was very fortunate. The surgery was so close to damaging my ability to speak.

The recovery at the hospital was very similar to the first surgery. In some ways, I knew what to expect. It was easier to recover. After being moved back to my room, I got up and walked as far as I could inside the hospital. I took pride in the physical condition I was in. I knew I could heal faster. The only side-effect that put me over the edge: level-eleven headaches. (Headaches are measured from one to ten, ten being the worst.)

I hit a point where I almost gave up my life for two days. I've never thought about giving up my entire life and no one should. There is so much a person can do. So relax in a quiet, comfortable place. Keep a positive attitude. Don't think; just rest.

I was so lucky to recover at my parents' house in Southern Arizona. I want everyone to know that it was hard as hell to survive the pain, but never give up because you will get better. I think some people do take their own lives before realizing they might suffer a little before life will get better. Healing is a process. Rebuilding is a worthy challenge. Life is an eternity.

It took a few days to get over the pain and to begin rebuilding my body and mind. By taking walks and stretching my body out every day, things began to improve. In fact, once I really started to get a good workout routine, I recovered fairly fast. Within five weeks, I was working again.

You just have to get over that hump and then life can move on.

Just a Note To Guess Who?

Today was my first work day after surgery.
Recovering from brain surgery has its own realm that is not
easy to deal with.
I have learned again that there is a reason why I am here,
to help people in any way I can.
I use my ability to talk to anyone and make them feel better
I love my life and look forward to death but,
I would like to stick around as long as you want me to God.
RS 4-7-98

Accept Death

Talk to people on the phone and turn around their feelings
Look at all the reality and explain life is revealing
Pass along all the changes you have been through
Encourage them explaining taking steps toward heaven is
true
We all must expect reality
Accept a positive fatality
Try to work along with everyone, especially ourselves
Live LIFE to its fullest, don't put life on a shelf
RS 4-7-98

July 4th, '98 "BANG" Bad Day

Celebrate, it's demanded
Have fun, it's a prerequisite
Not feeling good inside or out
Is breaking life's rules
Oh well, it's an unfortunate reality
RS 7-4-98 (Not feeling good)

Hanging On

Thoughts to change your mind confuse
Doubts and frustration diffuse
Decisions we must make each day of our lives
Affect us forever more
If you are wrong end the song
If you are right end the fight
If you are twittering on the brink
Then everything in life must stink
RS 7-4-98 (Confused)

Time Out!

It's time to understand
I've been thinking about it more and more
I could possibly know what is on my mind
Thoughts of all kinds roam throughout my brain
Probably no solution just the same
Is life a game?
Do we play until the game is over
Or maybe make the changes at half-time
RS 7-8-98

4/5 − 188

Dreaming, Screaming, Wondering and Wandering
For all I have within my personal sea
I wonder and wonder, Oh please forgive me
Thoughts and questions battle and hurt my mind
No answers fit none are kind
Shattered patterns of confusion abound
Horrible arguments make my head pound
Diminished, but not finished
Less or more, there is no score
Conclusions needed more and more
RS 7-23-98 (Lots on my mind)

Who Knows?

Pages of excitement surround my hands
Books of interesting thoughts engulfed my plans
Details and data fluctuate within my orbit
My game is about to begin again and I'm ready for it
Mismanagement accusations fly from within
Decisions are about to begin
Confusion reintroduces itself to me
No future action will take place you see
RS 7-25-98 (I just don't know anymore…)

I've Had Better Days

Bad days are bringing me down, all around
Disappointment, confusion, too much sound
My thoughts are wondering and wandering
Dreams pass in the distance, my mind is pondering
Decisions are here and there,
But with no answer within reach
Shedding my passion and excitement
Why do I have these moments…
What a way to teach
RS 8-6-98

Upset Deep Inside

Anger, frustration… bad vibration… bad situation
Hold back… don't let it go… don't let them know
Think about it first… you might be cursed…
Put … in a hearse
Daily mistakes… hearts that break… anger that shakes
Here we are again… suffering… feeling bad… feeling mad
No end is near… just lots to fear
RS 8-10-98

Turned 40 Today

NO, NO, NO… Where do I go
Decisions waiting to be discovered
But the answers were in the sky as they hovered
Do I fly away to review and input data
Must I move on and explore
walk out my door
Sleep in and snore
I don't know anymore
RS 8-24-98

A Moment In Life

Decisions, decisions, decisions
Changes
More decisions
Frustration, frustration, frustration
Changes
More frustration
RS 8-25-98

Another Day

So it's just another day
Work hard, then play
There is not a lot more to talk about today
And really nothing bad to say
I guess overall I've earned my pay
RS 8-26-98

Lights Camera Action
I interlude with passion
Don't Direct to Control
Let things go as they roll
The theme will slide
Go up and down then glide
Expose yourself don't hide

7-16-95

I do have my spirit
Can't always hear it
I purposely cheer it on
it's like writing a song

Confused About My Life

So what does one do when confusion takes over
Your mind is so tangled
Your feelings are fluctuating
Thoughts repeat, again and again
What do you say - how do you say it
There is no easy way to face reality
There is no easy way to accept the formality
The final presentation
RS 9-3-98

4/8 – 196

Our lives live on
There may be confusions with no solution
Balance can occur when realization appears
Understanding more about emotion is the key
Real life is good with emotional control
Love is so deep when it's in our soul
9-17-98

Wondering and Wandering

'Twas the night before decisions and
All through my mind not a creature
Was helping me figure out
What would be kind
I wondered and wandered
And all through my brain
Not a cell was cooperating
Which was driving me insane
When out from reality I heard a scream of disgust
Realizing my head would fall in the dust
I predicted the future and decided the outcome
When a large invisible creature yelled out that
"You are so freakin' dumb"
There is no easy way to decide a crucial fate,
One side or the other will be dominated by stinkin' hate
RS DEC 1, 1998 (Just wondering with a lot on my mind)

My First Poem For '99

A serious decision must be made each day
We constantly think about the role our journey may play
The length of reality related to our lives
Our long term results depending on our emotional
drives
Changes begin within our hearts
Diluted energy dissolving then starts
Our minds retreat from simplistic directions
Theories magnet human cross sections
This event becomes led with frustrating suggestions
Reality restores
RS 1-1-99 (Starting life again)

Life Is a Wonderful Disillusion

So it's time again to sit and think about where my
emotions rest
I contemplate the feelings and pray for the best
There is no actual reason to write this
Or think about my feelings
It's simply a moment in life
When questionable thoughts are revealing
A journey continues to release thoughts of confusion
Where am I going,
Where have I been,
Why am I encountering delusions
I want to put my heart on a stage and display each beat
I pray that joy takes over as I stand
And balance on my feet
As always confusion within my heart takes over
It's not very easy to understand or predict even though
I'm sober
RS 5-28-99

Dec. 24th, 1999 – A Dream – A Test

I'm in a huge church during a show
Time became different when I discovered what I
Wanted to know
Life was my journey, would I give or runaway?
I found out I was tested and realized what God had to say
You have to be able to donate your heart
And give your life away
Help another person, sacrifice,
Move on to heaven
That very same day
No questions or fear
Let go, let go, then God will be here
We are all on this earth for the very same reason
To celebrate with respect, every day and every season
A Christmas dream that spoke out to me
Give and you shall receive, let go and you shall see
RS 12-24-99

I Positive

Special people never leave your mind -
That is their wish.
*(I wrote this on a card to a friend about her husband dying,
their house and her memories 10-9-96)*

Millennial Surprise

Louisa ~ January 2000

One day in January of 2000, my doorbell rang. The last person I expected to see was the one person I wanted to see most. Russ said, "I was in the neighborhood." And he thought of me. He looked great, having cut his long hair. All those memories flooded back to my mind as if an emotional dam had burst. I softly shared with him that I was in a relationship and thought I had met "the one." Russ was still dating his longtime girlfriend. Sitting next to him on the couch, I was excited just to be in his presence. My heart wondered what could have been between us. But I had to put all those feelings back in the box. I had finally met the "one," or so I thought.

Things ended as quickly as they started with the person I was seeing and who I thought might be "the one." Not only was I heartbroken, but my father was diagnosed with Stage IV cancer on Valentine's Day. Life had a new sense of urgency. I felt an increased need to tell my friends and family how much I cared about them.

I found myself wandering through stores in need of retail therapy. As I looked at the jewelry and trinkets, I saw a cat pin made of twisted wire with a halo on it. Russ loved his cats and felt they had helped him through his healing process. I decided to change the wording on the tag from "Angel Puss" to "Angel Russ." I thought I would give it to him the next time I saw him. Weeks turned into months, and one night I finally called him. We met at a Borders Bookstore on Good Friday.

A Good Friday

Russ & Louisa ~ April 2000

A s I walked into my favorite bookstore, I spotted him all dressed in black, looking at the bestsellers with his back to me. I walked up and we immediately started our friendly, flirty banter. Looking for a place to sit, the only free chairs were in the children's section. Galaxy carpeting enveloped us. I gave him the cat pin and he loved it.

He was on a high. "My cancer is behind me. I beat it. I had my MRI scan this week and again clear pictures. I feel so good." His energy was so palpable – not a single reference to his death date. We moved to the café and I told him about breaking up with the guy I had hoped was "the one." I noticed how deeply and attentively he listened. When I finished, he looked at me and said, "Louisa, I have always loved you but was afraid of moving forward. I have broken up twice with someone because of you."

My breath paused, and then I said, "I have always had deep feelings for you, too." In that moment, cancer had lost its grip on me. It was something to be beaten, period. It's what I held onto so tightly for my father. People lived with cancer and they got beyond it. I had stepped across my threshold of fear. I looked at Russ and said, "I'm not afraid of the cancer anymore."

We walked into the parking lot and hugged. "I need to have a talk with Tina before we can begin," he said. I knew he was referring to his longtime girlfriend. I went home on a cloud, and later fell asleep in bed, replaying the first time we had met.

When I woke up, I had to figuratively pinch myself. Did that really happen? The one person I had known for years? I knew our friendship was special, but I really saw him in that moment at Borders.

First thing in the morning I checked my email. I found a message from Russ with the subject line *Time is Wonderful.* The message said, "Louisa, wow did that really happen between us last night?"

I replied, "Yes it did. I was trying to think when we met for the first time. Wasn't it Christmas of '95? I would love to see you right now and give you a big hug, and I would want it to be the first of many. I know I need to be patient. I would love to get to know you, go on real dates and, for me at my age, dating someone with the possibility of marriage. But, like I said, all in God's perfect timing."

The next day I received another email. Inside was a poem:

I went up to the mountain and what did I see,
A beautiful sun in the distance looking at me,
It was so bright and beautiful
I sat and opened my heart,
Knowing deep inside my life was ready to start.
- Rs

His email was filled with his thoughts, and I could tell he wanted feedback. Or was this my "ticket-out clause" that he wrote for me?

His message continued:

I hiked up Squaw Peak this morning at 6:30. I sat up on top and just enjoyed being up there. I was thinking about you and what we had talked about. I have this list in my head about myself to pass along to you to get some feedback. I work freelance, so I never know my work dates. I have the ability to do a lot of different jobs, but I am still not as smart as I used to be. I have to go to the hospital every three months for an MRI and meet with my doc. I am eight years past my 'death date.' I still have seizures every so often. I have to take meds 3x a day to keep from having one. I wonder if I will live for five or ten more years even though I know we could all go at any time. I think about my cancer and wonder if I could pass it along to a child. (That thought kinda goes with my overall confusion.) I wonder if I am good enough for a person that has so much for her future. I can't help that. I think about life in a different way only because my heart has been broken and beaten up before. I think about death as a step up to GOD and I am ready for it. I wonder too much, as you can see. I love to exercise, lift weights, and hike. I've never really camped but I'll try anything. I am still learning but I can't remember like I used to. I wrote some of this just to start to share some of what is on my mind. I meet with my Pastor on Thurs at 8am. Can we talk some more? I have to go to a shoot. I just got called. Please have a good day.

I wrote him back:

Good afternoon, Russ. I just received your email, wow that was very powerful. Here's a poem for you.

I met a man his name is Russ
He is a man who God and people trust
God gave him an awesome task
Russ needed to remove his mask
All that he had was removed from his life
His job, house, and even his wife
But God knew the plan
And that Russ was the man
Russ got brain cancer
So God made him a spiritual mentor
God sent Louisa to Russ
Laugh, cry with joy if you must
Because God had big plans for her to start
And he wanted him to accompany her heart

I see a man – a tall, gorgeous hunk whose outer beauty pales to the beauty inside. I see a man. I don't see a man with cancer. I see a man who did not let the doctors tell him his time, but rather God told him. I see a man who will live for forty-plus years and I will know till a ripe old age. I see a man who is not afraid of dying but who is afraid of LIVING!
I see you as a man who is a spiritual leader, and the jobs of now and the past do not define you. God has destined you for the work that requires all that you have – your emotions, your heart, your intuition, your listening ears. Look at what all the doctors said you would lose, and you did not. To say you're not as smart as you were is kind of dumb,

considering how wise you have become. The things your mind can't remember, the heart will not forget.

I see a man who is beginning to see his future again, and a girl who will take his hand and say, "Come dream with me again."

Still have doubts?

- Weez.

I wonder, as I look back now, where my words came from. Was I conduit for some cosmic intervention in this man's life? Or was it destiny that Russ and I would come together at this exact moment in each other's lives?

I waited eagerly for Russ's reply and was deflated by his response. He wrote that he needed more time to come to some final conclusion. He needed more time? He said he felt like he was back in school learning about life again, this time with his eyes wide open. Maybe I was the one who needed to have my eyes wide open. Maybe I needed to stop getting my hopes up high. Maybe that's far enough, Louisa?

The next day another email arrived:

My Pastor and I talked about a lot of things and it got real deep. I have several things that I need to do and it's not going to be easy. Many feelings were confirmed and it made everything straightforward but not simple. I am seeing so much more about life now. I'm looking forward to our first real date.

I appreciated Russ's words and his need for time and space. He was building trust with me as he moved slowly. Our lives had once again rearranged toward each other.

Our first official date was pie at a diner. I told Russ that I was getting baptized, and invited him. He said he would try to be there. (Translation: if he finally broke it off with his girlfriend.) As I was waiting to be baptized, a friend asked, "Hey is that your brother?" When I turned around, I saw Russ. I read my testimony and then was lowered into the baptismal.

We were inseparable after that moment and Russ brought an intentional presence with the moment. I noticed more sunsets, danced to more impromptu songs, and road his coattail of openness with strangers, little children, and the check-out clerk. He'd tell them we would have lots of tall children when they asked. He was very affectionate, a hugger who loved to hold hands. He would kiss me anytime, anywhere. He often joked at my resistance, saying, "Oh, someone is watching."

I headed back to the East Coast to be with my father, who was in a fight for his life. I went to a cabin with my parents and took the Lance Armstrong book, *It's Not About the Bike*. I know Armstrong has fallen from grace, but Russ really admired him as a cancer survivor. And for me, Armstrong's first wife sharing about marrying someone with cancer helped me put my doubts aside. My parents were curious as to why I had never mentioned Russ over the years, and they were about to meet him for the first time.

Precision Decisions

Life is so simplistic when you see it from an outside view
Everything seems easy, like when you're out in the pew
Comparatively, straightforward decisions are sometimes confusing
Understandably, when there has been unfair, sad, heart abusing
But things in your lives can change toward a wonderful dream
Even when it happens so fast, exhilarating our feelings, it may seem
When two agree to follow together their dreams can move on forever and ever
RS 5-9-2000

Carpe Diem

Can love start and stop and then take a side street
Not knowing where you're going or how to get there
Then, out of the blue, you collide
Your hearts wide open
Oh my gosh, life begins again
Hearts beat
Feelings Change
Drawn together for a Full Exchange
Then see if we can rearrange
RS 5-18-00

6-20-00

Life with Love is a gift
Finding someone will make a shift
Change your stride
Increase your pride
Rise up into the world you once left behind
See the wonderful treasure you did find
Renew all your dreams
Open the door
Live again like me
RS to L.M.P.S.

UP
AND
MANY

Life and death don't play with each other
There's just that fight from beginning to end
I guess when we least expect it, it happens
That rolling round and round, up & down crash.
Position is verified. Action begins or ends
Stories start Memories flow. Experiences renew
Feelings, now there's a tide wave. SPLASH!
Thinking about reality. Fatality. Escape
Spectrum of lives, people, matters and years
Sorrow. Sadness. Realization. Frustration
Goodbye, Farewell - Thank you - god Bless

RS 11-18-96 After Tonya's funeral

Will You Marry Me?

Russ & Louisa ~ August 2000

Here are excerpts from our journals from that time.

Russ

y birthday is in August and so much has taken place. I had been from the top of my life to the bottom, literally testing all my emotions. It was the Y2k highlight year and I turned another year in my forties. I felt comfortable and happy with my age since I am now close to eight years past my doctor's predicted death date. I felt strong, but I started the month with an MRI that created questions and finished six weeks later with another MRI that concluded a problem.

I have to tell you this month's story so you can ride the rollercoaster with me. It started with all the heat the sun can give to those of us who live in Phoenix, Arizona. July and August are hot! I had just found out the animation company that I got eighty percent of my work from had shut their doors and moved back to L.A. I was headed to Connecticut to meet my girlfriend, Louisa's, family. You don't know what to expect. They know a little about you from some pictures and descriptions. Inside my mind I was contemplating the best time and place to ask her father for her hand. First, her father had surgery scheduled in three days and second, I didn't know when would be the best time.

I shared what I learned through my cancer surgery and got to know more about him. The day before we were due to drive to New York for his surgery, I had just him and his wife in front of me and I started the conversation. It was strange to feel my hands all clammy, and I was looking for the right words. I said, "So if I asked you if I could marry your daughter, would I get your permission?" They knew I didn't have a job and they knew about my cancer. They brought up a series of questions and concerns for my health. I assured them I felt great. They both had deep hearts and love for their girl.

Louisa

After having returned from the supermarket, I overheard the end of a conversation in the kitchen. I heard my father say: "You don't need our permission, but you have our blessing. Your health okay? You sure you're up for it?" he said jokingly.

"Yes, I feel great," said Russ.

I walked into the kitchen, and Russ smiled at me.

Russ

Louisa's father was scheduled to have a fairly simple surgery, but that changed rapidly. We took turns staying with the family. We had taken a break and walked around New York City, and we returned to find the surgery wasn't completed. As we waited, the time dragged on to five hours, then six. A nurse came out to update his status and took such a negative position. We all started to lose it. The nurse's attitude pissed me off. No matter what the circumstances are, you tell the truth and keep a positive attitude. The time ticked slowly and the doctor finally came to talk to us. Richard had survived. As the doctor described what had taken place, we were all overwhelmed. Looking at the doctor's face, you could see he was tired and had really pushed himself to save Richard's life. That is a doctor with a deep heart. When Louisa's father was finally talking and feeling better, it was my turn to take his daughter away.

Louisa

Relieved by my father's improvement, my family encouraged Russ and I to take a break and to explore the city. We boarded the ferry for the Statue of Liberty. "Put your arm up like you're holding the torch!" Russ said. He loved having fun with the camera.

"Okay, Russ, look this way. I am going to take a picture of you," I said. He stretched his arms wide open like he was welcoming everyone to the Statue. He was never self-conscious. He liked pushing the bounds with me because he knew I didn't like bringing attention to myself.

We got off the boat and Russ grabbed my hand.

Russ

When we arrived I grabbed her hand and directed us away to the other side of the island.

Louisa

He led me away from the crowds, around the Statue, to a circular bricked area with a grove of trees.

Russ

I found a spot under a tree with no one close by.

Louisa

We sat on a stone wall and looked at the huge statue in the distance. There was no one around us.

Russ

It's not easy to ask the big question. I had such huge emotion deep inside my heart. I felt like a little kid when I started to talk to her. My voice squeaked, "Louisa."

Louisa

I knew what was about to happen, and my lips started to shake.

Russ

She looked at me, and I think she knew what I was trying to say as her lips started to shake. I finally got the courage in place and said, "Louisa, I love you so much. Will you marry me?" Her eyes became so shiny and bright and she said,

"Yes!" I had the ring in my pocket and slid it onto her finger. We hugged and kissed like little children in deep love.

Louisa

Trembling and excited, I finally said, "Yes!"

He took the ring out of his pocket and slid it onto my finger. We hugged and kissed like two young kids. It was five months to the day since we had started dating.

"Whew!" Russ said. "Boy do I feel good now!"

We ran back to the hospital to give my parents the good news. We went out for a special dinner with my aunt and uncle, who had come to visit my father in the hospital. Russ and I spent the next few days taking in New York City's sights. Then, on Russ's birthday, we got the special news that my father was ready to come home.

We decided to drive into New England where Russ's ancestors had settled the town of Winchester, Massachusetts in the 1600s. It felt like we were on a mini honeymoon.

Russ

I feel so much depth in a future wife I'm ready
I can't wait for the adventure
So much to look forward to
Who knows when it will take place
I see so much happiness on her face
I'm happy again more, than ever before
Her love and passion has opened that door
Feeling so deep in my heart
All these changes made life restart
8-17-00 RS

Louisa

Everything in our life felt right. We had everything we wanted. Russ returned to Phoenix for his scheduled MRI. I stayed behind with my father, feeling that is where I needed to be.

Russ

I flew home, and was scheduled for an MRI. These tests had become routine. This MRI showed a change on the brain. There was a line on my test. It was so hard to accept the truth, especially when it has such a negative aura. That they wouldn't come to any conclusion for another week made it worse. After years of clear tests, waiting was like being in an uncomfortable chair and you really want to get out, but it is just the beginning of a ten-hour meeting and you have no escape. Your basic slap in the face. It was so hard to tell Weez. I didn't want it to happen. Her spirit helped me so much. She was so positive and said, "Let's take one step at a time and find out what is going on."

Louisa

I wrote Russ a long letter, encouraging him, and he wrote me an email saying he would do whatever it took to fight. He felt frustrated and sad, but still lifted by my positive outlook. "I am going to make it through this," he said. "I believe things happen for a reason. I am so deeply in love with you. We will move ahead with things – marriage, kids, life. My heart has never been so sure."

After receiving this news, I wanted to be with Russ at his upcoming doctor's appointment. I told my father I needed to go home to really understand what was happening with Russ. It was hard to leave my dad, but he was doing well and on the road to recovery.

The Line

Louisa ~ September 2000

R uss and I walked up to a beautiful glass building
called Barrow Neurological Institute, surrounded by
symmetrical rows of red and yellow flowers that
surrounded statues of twisted metal. At the entry gate, Saint
Joseph greeted us.

We opened the door to the building and found a coffee
kiosk inside. Seeing the stand reassured me. The world was
still running fine; coffee was still being poured, just like any
other day.

One of us pressed the elevator button to go up for those
almighty answers. Little by little, as the elevator climbed, it
felt harder to breathe. Here I am again, yet another hospital.
We were only going to the third floor, but it felt
interminable. When the elevator dinged, my stomach tight-
ened even more. Ding! Ding! The doors parted. Signs and
arrows pointed us to all things neurological. New words, like
oligodendroglioma and astrocytoma now rolled off my
tongue, thanks to nights at the computer googling everything
related to Russ's diagnosis. I needed information before I
heard it from some doctor.

We opened the door to the waiting room. It was cavernous – the size of two sixth-grade classrooms. Any air I had left inside me was sucked out. I looked around the room and saw so many affected people. Feeling apprehension and anxiety, I looked at Russ, still with my naïve, grade-school crush. "He has to be all right," I said to myself.

I glanced at Russ, who looked perfectly healthy in my eyes, and then back out across the room. I registered people who looked in pain, and who had assistive devices. I saw sick people. The only healthy people were the ones waiting with them. We walked across the waiting area to the large windows, away from everyone, and waited.

Russ was a beloved patient of Dr. William Shapiro. Many staff members strolled out to meet us. Among them was Susie, a nurse. She was barely five feet tall. Light banter began between her and Russ. They quickly started talking about staying out of trouble. He was excited to introduce me as his fiancée. I smiled and did my best to join them, but kept one ear glued to the door, listening for Russ's name to be called.

"Russ Symmes." My stomach dropped as the door opened, revealing the path to the next waiting area. We entered a room with a desk, two chairs, and an examination table. Russ and I sat down and waited again for the doctor to come in. Dr. Shapiro was world-renowned in the field of neuro-oncology. I didn't know what to expect when he walked in the door. He was bald and looked as old as my father, which actually put me at ease.

"Congratulations on your engagement," said Dr. Shapiro. We then went across the hall to another room, this one about six feet by six feet, filled with white screens with pictures of Russ's brain. Despite my days in anatomy class, I was clueless. I looked at all the scans. I was looking for the good and bad areas. White on a scan was not a good sign. Dr. Shapiro pointed to one area and said, "This line is the area of concern." The line was white.

We returned to the examination room and I rattled off all the information I had gathered on Google. The doctor looked at me without dismissing me. Russ hopped onto the table for his neurological examination.

"Okay, Russ," instructed the doctor. 'Stretch out your arms to the side and bring your index fingers to your nose. Touch your fingers to each thumb." The reflex hammer came out next, testing his elbow and knee. I felt myself smiling with relief as Russ passed all these simple tests, not realizing the significance either way. Next came the questions from Dr. Shapiro. "Who is the President of the United States? What state do you live in? What is her name?" He pointed to me.

Russ answered all these questions with ease. I waited anxiously for the conversation to turn to the line on the MRI – the white line that gave everything in my life pause.

Dr. Shapiro hesitated to speculate as to what the line could mean, even though I probed. He decided that the best course of action was to have more tests. He also intended to bring Russ's case to the weekly team meeting with other members of his practice. It could be something as simple as radiation necrosis residue from past radiation treatments.

All I knew to do was to go into action mode and get back on Google. I wanted to know how soon we could get the tests performed, because all I wanted to do was to go out for dinner and a movie.

The next day I got an email from Russ, with the subject line, *Hello, Are you out there?* It was another poem.

Reassurance to My Fiancé

Oh my Weez. You will LOVE me and trust me, forever and ever
We will spend our incredible lives together
Adventures will build, passion will travel, excitement will abound
I desire you, your heart, your spirit and your trust.
Confidence and faith between the two of us is a must
I LOVE YOU RUSS xo

Something inside of me said, "Why wait to get married?" I stopped by his house and talked about what I felt. "Why don't we get married in a month?" I said. Russ was surprised. He took everything in, and then waited till the next day to give me his response. He said he would do whatever I wanted.

Le Chateau

Louisa ~ November-December 2000

The results of his PET scan quickly determined that the line on the MRI was the result of tissue necrosis in his brain from radiation damage. His doctor decided that, as a precaution, Russ should start a chemotherapy regimen. That November, he started a five-day cycle of chemo, with the only real side-effect being fatigue. He didn't lose his hair; he didn't lose weight. Life continued and I started a new consulting job.

As Christmas approached, my father needed another hospital stay to undergo a stem-cell transplant. It was the best course for him to be cancer-free and get into remission.

With this hope, my mom and sister continued to help me plan the wedding. We took a ride up to Le Chateau, a beautiful old mansion nestled in the Hudson Valley of New York. The stone exterior, hardwood floors, grand staircase, and elegant interior made it the perfect backdrop for a wedding. The outside stone-walled garden was covered with snow. I looked at the promotional album, which presented the Inn in all its seasons. We set a date for May 19, 2001. It would give my father enough time to recuperate. And with the news of a successful stem cell procedure, we all embarked on 2001 with much hope about the future.

I Do

Louisa ~ May 19, 2001

The worst thing that could have happened on my wedding day already had: my father passed away from cancer two weeks before. I thought of my dad and said to him, "Okay, Dad. I know you will be at my wedding. So between you and me, if you are there, give me a sign and lift my veil."

The drive to Le Chateau felt like an out-of-body experience as I sat with my bridesmaids and flower girls. When we arrived at the Inn, I stayed in the car and different friends peeked into the limo and snapped pictures. Even though I hated being the center of attention, I felt beautiful and special. My cousins opened the limo door, and their snapshots added to the nervousness that approached.

A friend handed me a small box through the limousine window, and said, "This is from Russ."

The card read, "With all my love to you forever, your husband in just a few minutes." As I looked at the small gold and sapphire cross, I was even more assured. The nervousness washed away.

Giant oak and red maple trees provided a lush backdrop to the garden. A stone wall, flanked in hanging green ivy, surrounded the perimeter of the yard. The view to the west looked upon the lush Hudson Valley. The white chairs were lined in ten rows of ten on the green grass. A white runner ran up the length of the aisle. White cascading ivy and tulle decorated the chairs of the center aisle. Pink and white azaleas draped over the sides of a stone altar, while glass candleholders flanked it. My mother had also ordered, without my knowledge, two vases of four-dozen white and blush-pink roses. I think she thought that the white represented my father and the pink represented me.

I Can Hear Now

There is a look
There is a sound
My feelings begin to abound
There is humor
There is care
There is mystery in the air
The future may have been resolved
RS- 1-6-95

Russ and I walked up to the altar and faced each other, holding hands as we listened to a friend sing a beautiful opening ballad. There was not a cloud in the sky and not a hint of wind. As I looked at Russ, so dapper in his suit, a gentle breeze came through the garden and my veil lifted and danced. Russ smiled as he watched my veil and I could hear gasps of delight from the guests as well. The wedding was bigger than both of us. In that moment, death and life met; grief and celebration kissed.

We didn't pick the usual wedding reading from Corinthians. Instead, I found a verse that my father had written down from Philippians 4:4-7, with his personal thoughts included. When his sister came to the front to read it, the birds started to chirp in applause.

She read, "'Rejoice in the Lord always. I will say again rejoice. The Lord is near. Let your gentleness be evident to all. Do not be anxious about anything, but in everything by prayer and petition and with thanksgiving give your requests to God. And the peace of God which transcends all understanding will guard your hearts and minds in Christ Jesus.' Think good thoughts and the God of peace will be with you."

Scriptures

On the way home today scriptures came to mind
Many different images appeared everywhere
Some were strange, some were kind
Relic movements abounded
The past revolved
Changes in ranges beyond consideration
Grown-re-growth taking place
Structure abounding on newness in this lifetime.
RS 12-97

Our Pastor, John, introduced our vows with affirming statements. Comically, we messed up. Russ stumbled over 'richer or poorer.' I went to put the ring on his wrong finger. "I'm sorry I've never done this before," I said. We both giggled.

John said, "You may kiss the bride." Russ kissed me long and deeply. As I felt myself topple, I leaned into him to prevent myself from falling.

Our first dance was to Don Henley's "Taking You Home." Russ first heard the words and said, "This is our song." Little did I realize how prophetic the lyrics would be.

SAD - GLAD - HAPPY

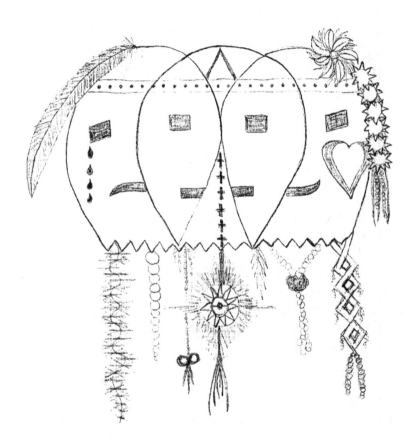

Russ lifted me over the threshold of our room at the inn. I had a special, long white-laced gown to wear. As I prepared for the obvious, I got nervous. It seems silly to me, as it was far from our first time. He motioned for me to sit down on one of the two oversized chairs near the bay window. I felt like he was hesitating, like there was something on his mind. I would find out later that he had pulled a muscle when he lifted me, and as he was in physical pain, he conveyed a seriousness that was not like the playfulness I had expected for our wedding night. He had written me a note the night before and wanted me to read it out loud.

Louisa, it is the night before we get married and I am here by myself, thinking of the life you and I are beginning. I have never in my life felt better about my future. There is an angel here with me telling me about the years we have together, children, and our incredible life we share. I love you like I have never felt before. I can't wait until 11:30am. When you read this, we will be married. Thank you GOD! Love, your husband, Russ.

I went over and sat on his lap and we seemed to stay there forever. He kissed me gently and then we headed towards the bed for some much-needed sleep. We waited till morning to do what newly-married people do.

The next morning, we returned to my parents' house. We entered on a high, but quickly remembered to dial down our emotions for my mother's sake. We opened all our wedding gifts that morning before leaving on the honeymoon. They came in all shapes and sizes, envelopes sealed in generosity and good wishes for our life together. We had canceled our Caribbean honeymoon in exchange for the Boathouse on the Cape and Nantucket.

The cobblestone roads of Nantucket greeted us as we came off the ferry. The island was unusually quiet. We pulled our suitcases up a quaint road. As we walked, we saw Main Street filled with charming shops and picturesque cottages. We turned toward the historic district and North Water Street to the Nantucket Whaler's Inn, once the home of a Whaling captain in the 1850s.

As we approached the front of the Inn, flowers dangled out of boxes above our heads. Our greeters sat in front of the small front door on the narrow steps. Two young, beautiful, and very chipper Irish girls escorted us through the private garden to studio number three.

Our beautiful room was steps away from town. We enjoyed our daily exploration and the simplest of pleasures: a slice of pie or a Maine lobster. People gravitated towards us and treated us so well. Russ and I must have radiated our love. His energy enveloped me. He was a gentle warrior who provided a place for my heart to heal and to grow. A door had opened in my life. I always wondered if I could trust myself in a relationship again, to fall crazy in love again, no hold-backs, and fully express everything that was in me.

Baby Blues

Louisa ~ Fall 2001

As fall approached, I had surgery to prepare us for a baby. We really wanted a child. We met with doctors before we got married to see if Russ's cancer and radiation had long-term effects. Urologist visits indicated that maybe, with time, there could be regeneration. It soon became evident that another course needed to be taken. While we were open to adoption, Russ was steadfast that he wanted a biological child. I gave him a lot of time to deal with the reality that, given all the tests, it would not be the case, and that we might need a donor. He was full of virility, but the simple fact remained: the cancer had diminished his sperm count and his ability to father biologically.

It felt great being married to Russ; we fell into an easy groove with each other. With the events of 9/11 and my father no longer with us, his love felt safe and secure. His health was good and we planned for the future. Always in the backdrop of our daily lives were the MRI tests every three months, the chemotherapy regimen of five pills monthly, and the associated blood tests. I never really worried about the white line on the MRI; the overriding emotion present was that Russ and I were living our life fully. End of story.

Changes. On. Off. Not For Sure

Say it the wrong way and pay a price
Finding out you're too nice
Make the changes you need to make for yourself
Number One in your life is not the husband or wife
 It's you – yourself focus on your own future
Add in another when the space is there
Don't try to keep the door open
They can knock and you can answer
Who is it? Would you like to come in?
The door is open
Just don't slam it…
(Post argument with Louisa)

This Is Real

Louisa ~ January 2002

In the beginning of 2002, I noticed that Russ's driving seemed different. He would overcompensate to the right. He also started to not book as many freelance jobs. He worked in the video and film industry, often needing to be on high ladders. He didn't share why he didn't take these jobs, and I knew he was overdue for his scheduled MRI.

One evening, as we went out for dinner, he asked me if I wanted to drive. We pulled into a gas station and Russ hopped out to fill the tank. I glanced at the side view mirror and my eyes widened as I saw Russ's body convulsing and foam coming out of this mouth. I got out of the car frantically yelling, "Russ! Russ! It's okay. Okay, hang on."

His jaw clenched down tightly and his head twitched up to one side. I knew the best thing to do would be to lay him down, but there was no room. Because he was so tall, I used the height of the SUV and leaned him against it. I started screaming, "Help me! Help me!" Wide-eyed strangers stared back at me. "He is having a seizure! Help me!" Someone brought me some orange juice, but I couldn't give it to him as his jaw was clenched. Slowly, the seizure started to subside.

I got him into the car and he asked me to take him home. As we drove out of the parking lot, the paramedics turned into the gas station. He didn't want me to stop and asked me to keep going. He kept saying he was fine. I felt shaken down to my core. How could this have happened? He was not fine.

He, on the other hand, was proud of what he had accomplished. My mother happened to call when we arrived home and, still shaking, I told her all the details. I found out later that Russ had decided to stop taking his seizure medications and he hadn't said anything. I was very upset. I told him to look at me. "Do you see how you scared me?" I asked.

Something shifted in me that night. This line on the MRI was real. This cancer was real. I had just seen the effects.

Retreat

Louisa ~ May 2002

Russ and I were open to all means of intervention – allopathic, naturopathic, energetic; we sought it all. In the first weekend of May, we headed to a workshop with Brugh Joy, an M.D. that left John Hopkins to pursue the transcendental.

We attended the workshop because we needed answers and healing. It felt way out of my comfort zone. Brugh Joy shared experiences, including how had he survived pancreatic cancer. In one of the exercises, he interpreted participants' dreams from the night before. Russ shared that he had a dream about diamonds. Brugh's interpretation was that Russ had mastered his heart chakra – an energy center of the body related to his cancer journey.

I also experienced a different side of Russ. He was always very intuitive, but that weekend I found him in conversations with like-minded individuals about reading auras and people's energies. My husband could experience many planes of existence, which was confirmed by his dream interpretation. Normally in large groups, he would be very friendly but quiet. I took away from the weekend that there was always a chance for a miracle or a remission.

As I look back on the time that I still had Russ, I realize I had my own apprehension regarding these new concepts: energy, aura, frequency, vibration, and chakras. I see now that they were all integral to the healing process; the spiritual, the mental, the emotional, and the physical planes all dance in accordance with each other and healing can be accessed at many levels. Russ immersed himself in healing with me as a witness. He was kicking cancer in the ass, or so I thought.

I would never imagine where and how that month would end, or that the torrential rains of cancer would begin again. I felt like Alice in some kind of nightmare. It happened so fast that I can't really remember the succession of who, what, or where came first.

The Monday after the workshop, Russ said, "My vision feels off." He had finally scheduled his MRI and the results were inconclusive. The line looked like swelling, not a tumor. It was located in his brain over his area of vision, speech, and motor. They couldn't do anything surgically because of the risk. We made appointments with a neuro-ophthalmologist and a speech pathologist.

The first guillotine came down with the neuro-ophthalmologist, who said, "Russ, the swelling in your brain is blocking a quadrant of your visual field. You do not have peripheral vision. This means you can't drive." He had been fortunate up to this time with his driving because only one quadrant had been affected, which I learned for the first time. The seizure, the swelling, all seemed to be connected.

I became very pragmatic when we got home. "Russ, okay, no problem. You can't drive. But there are services we can call until you get your vision back."

Russ loved to drive and feel the power of the wheel. He had given up riding motorcycles and he was resistant to the idea of giving up his car. And a convenient car service like Uber did not exist at that time.

The next day, we received a wedding gift from a dear family friend in the mail. It was a beautiful ceramic angel holding a purple box. She looked like Glenda in the Wizard of Oz. I took it as a sign that she was holding a gift from the divine.

The weekend of our one-year wedding anniversary, we headed to NYC for my cousin's wedding. Russ danced with my family, reassuring everyone. "Don't worry, I'm not going anywhere." I stayed positive, but kept inside what I really felt about his inaction.

We returned home and headed to the mountains for a weekend marriage retreat in a ridiculously small car we had recently bought. I drove, and Russ thought he was helping the situation by reminding me he was certified by the Mario Andretti driving school.

"Take your foot off the brake. Slow down with the accelerator instead. Pull your foot off," he said.

I couldn't wait for Russ to regain his vision and start driving again.

The two-lane highway heading north came to a dead stop. We waited and waited, and soon cars began shutting their engines down. One hour turned into two; traffic didn't move an inch.

As we waited, I didn't spare words, I just blurted, "I am afraid about losing you and you need to make a decision! Because if you don't, I'm afraid you're going to die." My body recoiled and he stroked my hair and listened intently, his eyes so warm and loving. He listened intently, as if he finally heard me, and agreed to make a decision. We arrived at the retreat and joked that our counseling had already happened in the car. The content of the retreat didn't seem relevant to us. We were living a different intensity and intimacy than those around us. Our conversations were concerned with life and death.

The men gave their wives a gift at the retreat. Russ gave me a silver frame with this poem:

165

On that special day I ran into the woman of my dream
She was everything I ever wanted yet we drifted
apart it did seem
Time seemed to move by yet we moved back
together once again
We might bump into each other while hiking Squaw
Peak
Go to hear music in Tempe although I wouldn't call
back in seek
Deep inside I knew you were the one
I tried to move toward you but was pulled back by a step
You were right there but the sun blinded me
Then that special day began to change our lives
My dream was to have us be husband and wife
It was that special Good Friday that started the journey
Listening to you drew me into your long travel...
To be married and more to heaven we shall soar
You are the one I have always looked for
RS 5-1-02

Russ began to reach for my right hand every night before
we went to sleep. Our forearms would touch as we looked
up at the ceiling. He would say, "Thank you God. I love you
God. I know we can make it through this."

Get Yourself Together

Louisa ~ June 2002

My focus shifted to Russ 24/7. He didn't need that intense focus, but I was between jobs and he became my full-time occupation. Everything shifted to how he felt emotionally, physically and spiritually.

I also learned about the areas of the brain – distinct areas right next to each other but with their own distinct jobs. One area controlled the ability to read to oneself. Another controlled the ability to read out loud. The doctors were trying to figure out whether the swelling was over his language or vision centers, based upon his symptoms.

Since his first surgery, he had mild symptoms of what is commonly called aphasia, when he sometimes struggled with word retrieval. He would have the word on the tip of his tongue, but would need to describe it until it came to him. He once said, "Louisa, do you know that thing, you know, the stars and stripes, that thing?" He was obviously trying to think of the word "flag."

He decided to occupy his time by writing a book about his journey, the words to which he couldn't even read on the screen now. He continued speech therapy at Arizona State University where he would work one-on-one with a speech pathologist. At the same time – it is hard to explain to people

– his cognition and his memory were totally intact. His verbal hiccups focused around his speech center where he had had surgeries and where the white line was located.

So when I shared with people the difficulty he had, it was hard for them to comprehend the situation. However, I grew used to the aphasia, which he had always had a touch of since I had known him; as husband and wife, we could read each other's minds.

I had planned a beach reunion with my friends. I was looking forward to our college reunion and returning to the Jersey Shore where I had many fond childhood memories.

When we arrived at the beach house, it was a relief to be with my friends and their children. But Russ's speech had taken a turn for the worst. He had a hard time making sentences.

One day, I came outside when he was backing the car out. My heart was in my throat as I quickly counted all of the children. Russ had decided to give them room for all their bikes. When he completed the task, I smiled at him with relief. I knew that for him, moving that car was somehow a small victory in the midst of his feeling out of control.

I wasn't ready to go on a downward spiral. The next day we woke up from a nap and I don't know what came over me. I grabbed Russ by the lapels and I said, "Get yourself together. Give me six more months!"

Surprisingly, that day, as we left the beach house, his speech returned to normal and remained that way. Every time I took care of myself, Russ would feel better and a shift would occur. For the first time, I recognized a change in energy, and I was able to conceptualize what that meant: energy.

Our life revolved around our trips to the MRI. Every three months, I held my breath as I went into that six-by-six room and looked at images on a screen. Russ stayed on his chemo cycles. He felt tired and nauseated, but there was no hair loss. He didn't look like a cancer patient.

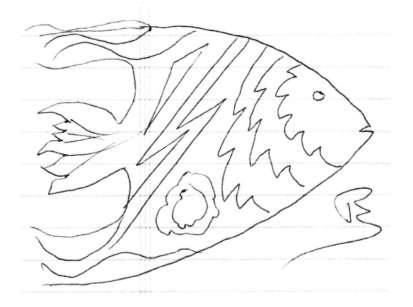

The Hukilau

Louisa ~ July 2002

We had a been singing a silly song for weeks: "We are going to HukiLau, the Huki, Huki, HukiLau. Everybody loves the Hukilau." We had a wish list of where we wanted to travel some day, and Hawaii was high on the list.

A Hukilau is a method of fishing invented by the ancient Hawaiians. The word comes from Huki, meaning pull, and Lau, meaning leaves. A large number of people, usually family and friends, would work together in casting the net from shore and then pull it back. The net was lined with ki leaves, which would help scare the fish into the center of the net. We were throwing our nets out and doing our best to scare the tumors into the center.

After we returned from the Jersey Shore, Russ's best friend, who worked in the travel industry, told us that he had an extra $125 round trip companion fare to Hawaii. He asked if we wanted to join him and his girlfriend. We jumped at this unexpected chance!

As I walked through the concourse in the Maui airport, I looked out the windows and saw the lush green hills in the distance. Excitement filled me for the first time in months.

My God, here we were in Maui, our Hukilau! The energy and enthusiasm in Russ were tangible. He had spent four years in Hawaii as a young boy when his father was stationed with the military there, and he always felt a strong connection to the Islands. The Big Kahuna felt right at home. I felt so grateful for this reprieve as we drove from the airport to our condo in Kihei with the trade winds rustling through the palms trees.

We had gotten the green light for this trip from his doctor. One of his former doctors actually practiced in Hawaii. The healing waters of Maui had an energizing effect on Russ. The return of his physical strength gave me an immense sense of relief. I was always worried about his safety, feeling more like his mother than his wife in recent days.

We did it all – driving the Road to Hana, hiking waterfalls and snorkeling. Russ was like a fish to water and on this particular snorkeling adventure we took a catamaran off the Island of Molokai. Russ eagerly headed into the water to snorkel.

I hesitated. I explained Russ's medical situation to the captain and asked if the crew could keep an eye on him. The captain told me about a healer on the island -- a Kahuna, a healing shaman. I watched Russ swim out until he was lost in a circle of colorful spaghetti floaters.

Over the loudspeakers our sarcastic crew said, "And for all you swimmers who are afraid of the water, we have floaties available." I smiled and decided to brave it.

Bright red- and orange-striped fish surrounded me. I felt unsure of myself in the water, my heart racing. I felt someone grab my hand. As I turned, I saw Russ, my Big Fish. Everything became calm, and we started snorkeling together.

"I'm going back to the boat. Please be careful," I said.

"I promise I will," he responded.

When I got back into the boat, I looked for Russ and again had lost sight of him.

When Russ came back on board, he was breathing heavily. He temporally lost his footing and fell, but got up quickly, laughing. He had a piece of driftwood in his hand – he had swum toward the restricted area. Something kept drawing him to it. Russ had always pushed the boundaries. Like the time he had gone over a cliff on a motorcycle. Somehow he had landed straight up. He had no clue how he survived.

We sat on the back of the catamaran with the winds blowing away white lines and MRIs. Cancer didn't have our attention.

"Russ, the captain told me about a healing Kahuna on the island. Do you want to find him?"

"Yeah, sure."

"You know, I was thinking. Maybe that's why we're here. For you to go to this healer."

He looked in my eyes and smiled with a kindness that put me at ease. Either way, we were here.

As we left the ship, the captain showed us where the Kahuna lived on the island. We followed the signs along the narrow, winding road toward the Shaman. Russ kept saying, "I hear him. He is saying everything is going to be all right."

Hawaii felt so good. I talked to Russ about staying and getting local jobs. He was doing so great. Why not live here?

"We could stay and look for our Blue Butterfly." (Pete Carlton was a ten-year-old boy who battled terminal brain cancer. His ultimate wish was to catch the most beautiful butterfly on earth – the rare Blue Morpho found only in the tropical rainforests of Central and South America. His mother convinced a renowned entomologist to take her wheelchair-bound son into the forest. Pete was miraculously cured after his encounter with the blue butterfly.)

With the blissful Maui trip behind us, we returned to where the grey area lurked – home. The neuroophthalmologist gave us the good news that Russ's vision had improved.

The realities of our financial situation came front and center. I needed to go back to work, but I didn't want to be anywhere but with Russ. This summer of unexpected vacations really gave Russ a boost and a distraction from all things he could not do. He threw himself into his writing.

The end of July neared, with no promise of employment in sight. I received a call from the company distributing my educational video series. They told me they had a significant order. I did the calculations and estimated that I would receive approximately $16,000-$17,000 in royalties. The next day, however, I received an email that I would actually receive a check for $46,400. The house I grew up in was number 46. I took that as a sign from my father.

Russ also learned that his disability compensation was going to be reinstated. This was a miracle. We were elated and started to dream about the future.

Surprise Big Kahuna

Louisa ~ August 2002

While in Maui, I bought a notepad shaped like a man's blue and white aloha shirt. I thought it would make a great invitation for Russ's 44th birthday party at the end of August. I decided to throw a surprise Hawaiian luau with everyone in Hawaiian attire for the Big Kahuna's birthday.

It looked like we were headed for a remission after all. The latest MRI showed everything was stable. It was the best birthday news to receive!

Our friend, Rachelle, opened her beautiful home overlooking the Valley to us. My friend, Chuck, an amazing amateur chef, prepared the feast. I spared no expense for the party: shrimp, Hawaiian roast pork tenderloins with habanero prickly pear sauce, and an amazing antipasto spread.

The September MRI showed a spot of concern for the doctor. I saw no signs of change in Russ. His speech was fine, his balance straight, and his strength undeterred. Just like everyone commented at the birthday celebration, Russ was holding his own. But he did have one new symptom: a numbness in his hand like it was falling asleep. Dr. Shapiro suggested adding a new drug to the regimen, Tamoxifen. The drug added another $1,000 to our monthly medical bills.

Still unable to read the computer screen, Russ continued to write his book. Daily therapies occupied his time. Thank God it was football season. He had season tickets to his beloved alma mater ASU. He was a Sun Devil through and through who never missed a game.

Scrambled Numbers

Louisa ~ September 2002

Scrambled numbers were the next a la carte symptom to appear as we headed out for my birthday dinner in late September. A friend had called to sing "Happy Birthday" to me and was concerned because Russ had made no sense. Not only were his numbers being affected, but he couldn't retrieve the right words he needed. I told him, "just keep talking," playing a game of charades.

We drove to the top of North Mountain to a scenic restaurant overlooking the Valley for an expensive romantic dinner made possible by a gift certificate from friends. Walking up the beautiful stone steps, I noticed his balance was a little shaky.

Relieved to make it to the table, the expansive city of lights brought a wave of memories. The last time I had been here was for a Father's Day brunch. I looked at Russ, tears welling up in my eyes and streaming down my face. The waiter approached and stepped back, careful not to intrude. Maybe he thinks Russ is breaking up with me. Would this be my last birthday celebration with Russ?

As if he could read my mind, Russ looked at me so deeply with those beautiful blue eyes and smiled. He squeezed my hand even harder to reassure me. But I could see a difference in him.

Despite the tears, we had an enchanting night. As we descended the four steps to leave the restaurant, he became unsteady. I gave him my arm, providing the best steadying hold I could muster. Russ was a tall and strong guy. I wasn't very strong. I swear, I don't know where strength comes from sometimes.

I felt that I was the only one who was responsible. I know this is not true now, but it didn't occur to me that I could reach out to others. Why wasn't this obvious to me? To others? People can't see. Can't you tell the guy is struggling? Can't people see I need help with Russ?

Russ and I never were part of a core group. We had friends and family all over the country. We just endured the storm together. It felt like rain hitting you in the eye while trying to steer the barge through the torrents, hoping Russ didn't fly off the deck. If I had children to care for during this time I would have lost my mind! Or maybe more people would have stepped up to help.

My sister was getting married in December. Heading to Connecticut for her bridal shower felt like the great escape. I needed a break, even if for a few days. Afraid of leaving Russ alone, I suggested he stay with his parents. He didn't want to be driven three hours to be "babysat" by his parents. He wanted to be at home, and he assured me he would be fine.

Let It Be

Louisa ~ October 2002

It was fall in New England, and it was great to be with my cousins for the bridal shower. They all asked me how Russ and I were doing. He was never a minute away from my mind. I worried about him, and he constantly told me that he missed me, too.

Once when he called, I said, "I don't miss you." I wish I could take those words back. I know that it was a mean thing to say. I didn't miss the storm. I was on a dry island. In my absence, his friends were supposed to stop by to check on him. But I had a feeling that they called to check in on him and he simply waved them off.

Fortunately, his longtime buddy David did go by and was really concerned. He called me. "Louisa, you need to get back here. He is not doing good. He took a serious fall down the stairs."

I got home close to midnight and immediately went upstairs. When I reached under the covers to hug him, he felt so frail. The next morning he showed me the marks on his back where he had fallen. Our twenty stairs had become a hazard.

We had a long talk about what I said about not missing him. He was hurt. "I am sorry," I said. "It's not about you.

It's about the cancer. I am sick of this. It's so hard. I can't help you up these stairs anymore. I can't watch you 24/7. I can't try to understand what you are having trouble saying. I just needed the break. That's all."

I didn't feel any alarm to call his doctor about his fall. When I came home, his strength seemed to improve, and the feeling and strength in his left side returned. Something deeper shifted in me. I was now afraid to leave him alone. Period. I would call him on my cell forty-two times when I was away.

We were scheduled to see another specialist, Dr. Dang, an acupuncturist. I was running around frantically, looking for the next solution.

One of Russ's best impersonations was of his favorite Beatle, Paul McCartney, so when his "Back in the U.S." tour came through Phoenix, I bought tickets. I needed a distraction.

As we walked toward the arena three blocks from the car – a distance which now felt like a mile – Russ leaned heavily into my body for balance. His right foot dragged. In that jovial moment, I felt anything but light. Once again, the cancer made its presence known.

I had called ahead to my friend, Scott, who worked at the arena, and requested accessible seats. Our seats faced Stage Right. I felt so relieved to have Russ seated. There was a red curtain in front of us, and only a microphone stand in view. I said, "Russ, at least we can see the mic."

When the curtain finally went up, the stage was expansive. We could see everything. I could see Paul McCartney and feel his boyish charm. I was close enough to be a participant of an exchange of energy that belonged between him and his crowd. That energy was electric. Once again, the curtain pulled back, and dancers holding big decorative hearts emerged, encircling the stage and aisles.

The music blared with the Beatles, Hello, Goodbye. Paul's song overflowed with the love that he embodied. Russ looked at me with a huge smile and high-fived me. For three hours, we were immersed in our love submarine, buoyant and navigating through cancer's storm. The tribute songs to John, George, and his late wife, Linda, made me think about my father.

As Paul sang those familiar words about times of trouble, I included my own version:

Father Richard speaks to me
Let it Be, Let it be
There will be an answer.

I wished I could pick up the phone and speak to my dad. As much as I enjoyed the concert, I couldn't deny what was happening to Russ. Something more was wrong with him.

Lost in my thoughts, I kept turning my attention to the show, and to the normalcy of the moment. I told myself we were living like everyone around us in the arena. My husband was on a high. I swear when Paul waved to our section, he looked right at Russ.

Russ's energy and spirit were so lifted as we left the building, but his ability to walk seemed much worse. He leaned even more heavily on me, and dragged his foot. His 6'6" frame was too much for me to handle. I could feel the people's stares as we walked back to our car.

I said, "Russ you need a cane. I can't handle your weight."

He said, "I have one in the garage."

The "cane" looked more like a hiking stick. He was reluctant to use it, preferring to walk around and balance himself with the walls, door frames, or me. Russ was a stubborn guy – very gentle, but very prideful in his physical prowess. Though weakening physically, he had always been an athlete to the core. He pushed himself to the limits.

One day we took a walk down to the community mailbox together. It was a long distance – about a quarter of a mile. When we got to the mailbox, he pivoted and almost fell. If I hadn't been there to catch him, he would have fallen. Days later, I came home to find the mail on the couch. I knew that he had gone to get it but I still asked, "Who got the mail?"

"I did."

"You did? You walked to the mailbox by yourself to get the mail?"

"Yeah."

I was amazed by his stubbornness and his unwillingness to be stopped.

Early the next morning, I heard a loud bang. I turned to Russ's side of the bed. It was empty. I sat up and heard a struggle just outside our bedroom. I headed towards the bathroom and saw Russ lying in the entrance of the door.

"Russ, Russ, are you okay?" I saw a burn mark on the side of his face from where he slid against the wall, trying to prevent his fall. "What happened?"

He was so dazed he could not even explain it to me. His body had just given out from under him. I asked him to wake me and he told me I was hard to wake up.

I began to sleep with one eye open. We had an upcoming appointment with his doctor so I didn't feel alarmed to call right away. But, the next day as we drove home from his acupuncture treatment, he started to have a seizure. I pulled over. In the safety of his seat, he struggled until the seizure stopped. It lasted a long time. I called his doctor, then the MRI scheduler, explaining the urgency. The next day I had appointments with both. I knew he was taking all his medicine, unlike the last and only time I had seen him seize at the gas station.

Without A Plan

Louisa ~ November 2002

The skies looked like dense, gray cotton balls as we waited in Dr. Shapiro's office. Russ struggled with his cane as he entered the building. He needed a wheelchair. I knew he was very resistant to the idea. I encouraged him that it could help with "long distances."

His father was in town for a meeting and joined us for the doctor's appointment.

Dr. Shapiro normally looked at the MRI with a quiet and methodical approach. But today he screeched, "What!" He was shocked at what he saw – a huge tumor mass in the cerebellum.

We stood in this three-by-three-foot room looking at the MRI in disbelief. We all stared at the screen. "What about..." I began to spout out alternative therapies I had read about. I was still in action mode. His father asked about the cerebellum, and Dr. Shapiro explained that it controlled his gait and balance.

I said, "I think Russ needs a wheelchair, walking is getting difficult for him."

Dr. Shapiro was speechless and without a plan. We couldn't do chemo because Russ' blood count was so erratic. We had never seen Dr. Shapiro at such a loss like this before.

I could tell that he really felt bad that he didn't know what to do. I remember saying an awkward thank you when we left his office. I could feel the dour looks of the nurses as we left.

When we arrived home, Russ called his mom and his siblings. We all were in a state of shock.

I said, "Russ, do you want to know?" I wanted him to know whatever he needed to know. We never talked about him dying. It was the elephant in the room that was never spoken about or acknowledged. He said no.

The bell dinged as we opened the door to the wheelchair showroom. An assortment of assistive devices surrounded us. Russ first went to a small, sporty-looking wheelchair. But due to his size, he needed a standard one. I could see the defeat in his eyes. When we returned home, he asked me to keep the wheelchair in the car.

He insisted on doing everything on his own, with his right arm basically dangly at his side. The tumor had affected his muscle tone on his right side. He balanced using his left side. I gave him space, but intentionally hung out upstairs until he was ready to go down. After his last fall, I was afraid of the stairs but I didn't want to let on. It was a thirty-foot drop from the top of the stairs to the bottom. I worried he would lose his balance and fall over the banister from the second floor.

We settled into the simple things. The plan was to wait until Russ's blood counts evened out before doing another cycle of chemo. It was November in Phoenix, and the weather was unusually beautiful – in the 80s. We sat and looked onto the golf course, listening to the birds. I had just done a round of fertility treatments, and hoped I was pregnant. The only medications Russ was taking were steroids for swelling in the brain. His face was getting puffy but I hardly noticed. All I saw was that we could get over this speed bump and get back on track again.

As Thanksgiving approached, we planned to visit his parents and go to the rival University of Arizona vs. Arizona

State University football game. Russ cherished this tradition. He had played football for ASU and this was one part of his identity no one could take away from him. He had season tickets and still insisted on going to every game. One Saturday I said, "I'm sorry Russ, but I can't take you to the games anymore. It's too hard." I could tell he was disappointed. Not even five minutes later, his best friend, Blaine, called and asked if we were going to the game. He took Russ to the rest of the games with special golf cart access to his section.

My mom grew concerned as I relayed the news about Russ's deteriorating health. She was in Connecticut and could see how rapidly Russ's health was deteriorating. "Can you get someone to help?" she asked. "Are there special services available?" No one used the word hospice – not even Russ's doctor.

I started to get anxious. The last thing I wanted to do was drive three and half hours to his parents to celebrate Thanksgiving, but Russ insisted.

We got special, accessible seats for the football game. I felt like his protector. His parents were on the opposite side of the stadium. Everyone was doing their best and we were being strong for each other. Russ wore his ASU hat and he raised his left arm when there was a touchdown. I remember watching him with a familiar sadness; I had seen it before with my father.

At one point during the game, Russ needed to use the restroom. He needed help to get out of the chair and into the men's restroom. I felt so helpless. But then a kind stranger opened the door and Russ was able to navigate inside.

Russ snapped back to his old self when we returned to Phoenix. A surprise visit from his sister and niece to hang Christmas lights let us feel hope, if only for moments, in the background of the unknown. We had a dinner reunion with some of his ultimate frisbee friends. I noticed them talking loudly to Russ, whose difficulty with walking and talking made everyone uncomfortable.

We decided to keep things low-key except for a tradition of Friday night movie night. He felt strong and wanted to go. We turned the corner into the darkness of a packed stadium-seating theater. As we whispered in hushed tones, he pointed with his cane. "There are some seats."

"Where?"

"Up there." He indicated the very top row. I held my breath, knowing that if he lost his balance, we would both give this audience an action scene to remember. Carefully – lifting one foot and then dragging his left foot – he made it, his warrior courage rising again and again.

Green Acres

Louisa ~ December 2002

I kept hearing "Here Comes the Sun" from the Beatles, and I had flashes of a cemetery scene. One day on the way to his acupuncture treatment, I asked him if he was planning his funeral. He asked me if I wanted to see the cemetery that he had chosen a long time ago, as it was near the doctor's office.

We turned into Green Acres Cemetery, which looked like a huge football field. It was unusually green for a desert cemetery. He told me that he chose it because of its proximity to the ASU football stadium. He could see the lights and hear the fireworks on a touchdown.

I laughed and loved him even more in that moment: always a Sun Devil. We drove to the back of the cemetery to the Mausoleum area. It was underground. I looked up at a huge wall with tiny name markers. They looked liked little license plates that hang on the back of a kid's bicycle. It seemed like a cold and impersonal way to pay respects to your loved one.

We walked through another section of the cemetery to a beautiful garden, with chimes in the trees and a fountain. I asked him if I could change things. He agreed, and again we never talked about "it" – the big "D" word. That night as we crawled into bed, we looked at each other and both broke down crying. We just rolled towards the middle and hugged each other.

He didn't want to know the "it." He had thrown out time a long time ago. He was now ten years past his original diagnosis of three months. No one was going to tell him his time.

The next day as we waited again for Dr. Shapiro, Russ motioned to me. "Move your chair closer." I inched my way toward his wheelchair. Susie, his favorite nurse, came out with her usual pep talk to not give up, to stay strong. Russ gave her his usual spiel, but I could tell he was just going through the motions – the banter of dead hope hitting the net again and again in a match we were losing.

I, on the other hand, was engaged in a conversation with a much older woman. I smiled at her with a weak politeness, as I had one ear on the conversation between Susie and Russ, not really interested in idle waiting-room chatter. She said, "It's not easy being a caregiver."

"I'm his wife," I replied. "I'm his love-giver." I hated the word caregiver. This was my husband and I was loving him the best I knew how, with every fiber of my being.

We wanted the okay to travel. I followed Russ's lead, but maybe I was being naive. I asked Dr. Shapiro if Russ could fly. His concern was more about the strain on me and that it may be physically hard to bring him back. Russ's platelets had us in a holding pattern, with no chemo until they rose again.

Dr. Shapiro had found a way into our hearts a long time ago. In one of our first meetings he candidly said, "You're like my kids. I'll tell you what to do but you'll do what you're going to do." He was our Superman, using all his might with his drug therapies and clinical advancements. Russ had given him a Superman shirt on one of our visits. I liked his honesty. He treated us like people, not like patients.

My sister's wedding was fast approaching, and I didn't want to miss it. I knew I couldn't leave Russ alone either. I had an overwhelming feeling that it was just him and me. I didn't tell him that there was a chance we would not attend the wedding.

I knew we needed help and solutions with his situation. His balance was getting worse, and I didn't have the physical strength to make it work. I was bored with the tedium of our situation. I ordered super cable with 400 channels so we could have anything on demand. The day-in, day-out stress was building; I loved Russ so much but I needed help. I didn't know where to turn for resources. I didn't know what to look for or where to start to find what I needed.

That Friday was not so good. Russ fell again in the middle of the night. He was too weak to go anywhere and he couldn't speak. He looked at me and mouthed, "Nothing is coming out." The swelling had moved over his speech area. He stayed upstairs in the loft all day. There was no way he could make it down the stairs.

Russ's melancholy remained all day. I asked him a million times, "Are you okay?"

I picked up the phone and called our Pastor, John. He and his wife, Stacey, asked if they could take us to the movies for our Friday night tradition. Russ was too weak and declined the offer.

John said to us, "You don't know how long this will go on, so make memories every day. Just sit or do little things." They sat with Russ while I ran out to get a movie. I also picked up a meatball sandwich and a newspaper. It felt strange to do something so normal. It was like I had re-entered the real world for a moment.

We sat next to each other on the couch watching Mr. Deeds. It was a stupid comedy, but just what we both needed. Russ put his arm around me and pulled me close, like a first-date move. I leaned my face into his chest. For two hours, it felt like my guy was holding me. With renewed vigor, he stood up and walked across the room. Startled, and hoping this was a good sign, we giggled.

His voice came back on Saturday. He was on the phone when I woke up. "Hello momma." His parents had begun to call daily. I put them on speaker when Russ couldn't speak. We called it the Fog. As soon as it came, it left again. He stayed on the phone for two hours, and then he wanted to go to the 50th birthday party of our friend, Rachelle, that night. From the first time they had met, they had a special bond.

I resisted his desire to go to the party. He wasn't strong enough and he couldn't even get dressed. He asked me to bring him all his stuff – his toothbrush, razor and clothes. Everything was getting harder because the right side of his body was totally dead weight. He compensated, though, finding a way to manage with only the use of his left arm and leg.

The transfer from the wheelchair to the height of the SUV was hard enough, but when we got to the party the driveway and sidewalk were packed with cars. I rolled into the house with the wheelchair and it felt like I was bringing in an alien. To be honest, all the party members looked like aliens to me now.

Rachelle's children came over, and then more people came closer as we settled in. Russ looked at me with sweetness and vulnerability. We exchanged looks as I got up and down to make sure the night air from the patio was not too cold on him. He smile returned, and he was happy to be there for his friend.

I worried about him getting up the stairs when we returned home from the party. Amazingly, he made it up the stairs. But when he got to the bathroom, he began to lose his balance. I ran to get to the wheelchair. When I returned, he was on his back on the floor. My only suggestion was to get the next-door neighbors to help. He asked me to wait, and then he grabbed the door frame and lifted himself up with his left arm. We both looked at each other in amazement.

Silently, I said to myself, "God, if you're going to take Russ, take him fast."

A friend stopped by after Russ fell asleep. I told her I had intense chest pains. It felt like my heart was going to break open.

Russ wanted a huge breakfast on Sunday: eggs, oatmeal and pancakes. He sat quietly, wrapped in afghans, and watched his favorite football teams play. His mood was sad again. I wheeled him out to the porch to look at the green grass. My mom called and spoke to him. I could hear him put on a happy voice.

A friend returned from helping me with errands. She had beautiful lilacs. "These are from Russ," she said.

I had had enough of football. As evening approached, I lit candles around the loft and put on some music. I pretended to dance around the room like a flirty ballerina. I came close to him. "How about some kisses?" I kissed him softly on his cheeks. Due to his weakened state, we had started this sweet exchange of cheek kisses in recent weeks. In the midst of this exchange, he surprisingly pulled me to him and kissed me on the lips with all his strength. He laid my head on his lap and he gently stroked my hair. We stayed that way without saying a word.

It's a cool summer night
perley clouds drift in the breeze
good feelings sourround me
   Slashing and dashing in the tree
Deep in my heart confessions
      (ABIDE?)   abides
   Still lonely and protecting
that's why my heart still hides

                    7-30-95

Reality is so hard
Convince yourself it will all work
Deny the down and the doom
   Will anything happen
      Very late or so soon ?

{ Unveriable is terriable }
                X 10
            TIMES TEN

Don't Let Him Go

Louisa ~ December 9, 2002

I fell asleep to the Sopranos and woke up to no response from Russ. Normally our days would start early, but this morning I had overslept. Immediately, I knew something was wrong. He was in and out of consciousness, almost like he was drugged. I dialed 911. Then I called Stacey, and Martha, a nurse who was a stranger to me but a member of our church who left a message to contact her if I needed help.

At the hospital, we were shuttled to a small room with four blue-curtained cubicles. Doctors shuttled in and out, asking me the same questions. "What meds is he on? What happened?"

One doctor came in and looked closely at Russ and said, "I know Russ. We used to work out at the gym together. He's a great guy." This acknowledgment lifted me in the moment.

I thought to myself, "Yes, he is a great guy so please fix him. Don't let him go." As he lay on the gurney, he kept having more seizures and going deeper and deeper into a state of unconsciousness. Exhausted, I was happy to be near immediate medical care.

The busy ER staff was trying to line up a CT scan and a brain scan. But the brain scan tech was nowhere to be found. As long as Russ had brain activity, we were moving forward.

I waited with Stacey. At one point, she went to get me a sandwich. I was alone and frustrated that nothing was happening. I decided to check his eyes. I had enough medical training to assess acute medical signs. I lifted the lids of his eyes. One of his eyes was normal and the other was totally dilated like he was dead.

I rushed to find the nurses and told them what I had discovered.

"We'll be right there. Try to rouse him." I went back into the room, grabbed Russ by the shoulders, and shook him as hard as I could. "RUSS! RUSS!" Nothing. No response. I knew this was not a good sign.

His parents finally arrived as evening approached. I thanked them for being there. I updated them, and my mother by phone. The doctors came in and moved him into another room in the ER. It was bigger and brighter, with just one bed and a door.

I was greeted by another doctor, who was extremely tall like Russ with deep-set and caring eyes. He looked at me, and I knew he was doing everything he could. But then a very short Asian woman doctor came up to me, snapping questions. "Does he have a living will? Did he sign a DNR?" The answer was yes, but I wanted to know if he had brain waves.

He did; they had finally located the brain tech. My Pastor, John, joined me at Russ's bed. I watched Russ twitch. I began fearing the worst. I knew it was a sign of deep neurological irregularities. I opened my Bible and looked at John and said, "I don't have anything left in me." John said the right thing, which I can't remember.

I thought back to my prayer the night before, after Russ lost his balance, when I asked God, "If you are going to take Russ, take him fast."

I pushed the ICU button, but was told I would have to wait in a cavernous waiting room as Russ was being attended to. I sat in the dark room, and then moved to a big chair in the hallway facing the ICU doors.

The elevator bell dinged, and out came Rachelle and her boyfriend. I was so surprised to see her. We waited together until we could see Russ. We entered his dark room, lit dimly by an overhead light. He was on a ventilator. The hissing of the machines filled the room. She asked me if I wanted her to stay, and I said I was okay. I pulled up a chair next to his bed. "I know Russ. I know Russ this is it."

It had arrived. The moment. It was our moment. As I sat and listened to the machines, I knew he was already gone. I sat next to his bed and cried and cried.

At 2:30am, I knew it was 5:30am on the East Coast. I went downstairs to the empty lobby and called my mother. My voice broke as I told her things were not good. She got on a plane that morning.

I then went to the hospital chapel, but it was closed. I went out the wrong door and found myself locked outside. Christmas tree lights lit the way to the security office next to the main entrance. I explained my situation and the gentle security officer escorted me to the chapel doors, unlocking them. I went inside and prayed. My last attempt. For what, I didn't know. A miracle?

Morning arrived, and Russ was scheduled for a 6:00am MRI. Dr. Shapiro came in. "The tumor has herniated and it is pressing against the brainstem. When we take him off the ventilator he will stop breathing and go."

I was in peaceful acceptance – or numbness – as if I had prepared the night before. I thought now that the most difficult part will be to tell Russ's parents.

Russ's surgeon came to see him and told me he was such a special guy. I knew it was going to be hard to tell Russ's parents. I got on the phone and started calling close friends.

The day was like a scene out of a movie. His friends tentatively came into the room and I said, "He can hear you." There was an atmosphere of love as we laughed and cried, strangers gathered in oneness.

My mom arrived in the afternoon. We all agreed that the next morning, we would remove the ventilator at 8am.

Amazing Grace

Louisa ~ December 11, 2002

The bright, red-orange sunrise came through the corner window. The sounds of the ventilator were interrupted by short repetitive breaths coming from Russ. I worried that the end may be coming sooner than expected. I called John to tell him what was happening and he asked me to check with the nurses to see if this was unusual. I went into the hallway and Lani, the traveling nurse from some Gaelic land, felt like an angel to me now. Her soothing voice calmed me and told me that what was happening was normal.

One by one, family members came in and surrounded the bed: Russ's parents, my mom, his brother and wife, Blaine and his wife. John, Pastor Staats (Russ's Lutheran Pastor), and Sister Judith (my former Catholic boss), rounded out the spiritual circle.

Russ's father motioned to me and asked me where I would like to be. I was at Russ's left side. He motioned for his wife to join him at the left but she stayed at the bottom of the bed.

Nurse Lani was across from me. John asked if anyone would like to say anything. My mom requested the Our Father and Russ's dad recited a poem. Sister Judith sang Amazing Grace.

Nurse Lani started to remove the adhesive tape off the ventilator. I said, "No, no, no." I thought his passing would be quick. I asked her to be careful with the tape as he had a mustache. He started to breathe, and then my mother covered my eyes. I knew there were parts of death she didn't want me to see.

Slowly, he continued to breathe and turned his head to me. I didn't know if this was a reflex or an intentional movement. I told him who was in the room. I named everyone, and then I noticed a new nurse. I told him he would have loved Lani and her Scottish brogue, as I imitated one myself. I told him it was okay to go. I told him we would miss him but it was okay to go. I told him of all the things that were waiting for him. I told him to say hi to my dad.

Then he took a deep breath, which felt like a confirmation he had heard me. Slowly, for twenty minutes, he continued to breathe. And then, moment by moment, we watched his heartbeat become slower and slower until the line stopped off the screen.

Instantly, I was enveloped in a beautiful peace. Wherever he was, I felt this beautiful peace. As soon as his heartbeat stopped, I exited the room into the hallway.

We moved to the waiting room and began to talk through funeral plans. Pastors Staats and John planned the church service. I was looking forward to going home, as I hadn't slept in three days. Every time I thought about Russ, I would hear him in an exuberant voice saying, "I am so happy, Sweetie Pie."

A representative from the funeral home arrived to discuss what Russ had chosen for his burial. "He chose a blue casket," he said.

"A blue casket?" I knew that he loved Elvis. Maybe that's why he chose it. I wanted to see it, or maybe change it. The representative asked me to come to the funeral home and bring the clothes I would like him to wear. Standing in my closet with my friend, I picked out his favorite blue shirt that he said brought out his blue eyes, a sport jacket, dress pants, and his favorite tie that belonged to my father.

They opened the casket showroom floor. The whole scene seemed so surreal. And there was the bright blue casket. The funeral director then informed me, "We checked, and the casket does not come in a size that will fit Russ." Inside, I sighed with relief. I changed it to a more neutral color.

After we left the funeral home, my mother, sister, and I headed to Green Acres. We walked the cemetery and I picked out a new section near the fountains and chimes in the trees, where I could sit next to his grave.

I didn't announce Russ's death to anyone. I couldn't say the words, "Russ died."

My siblings arrived from all around the country. I was really touched that my sister-in-law and soon-to-be brother-in-law also made the long trip. Friends and family made calls for me, and they did a great job of screening my calls. They told me the caller's name, and if I felt like talking, I gave them a signal and they handed me the phone.

Mementos from Russ's life surrounded the funeral room: framed photos, ASU memorabilia, and array of exquisite arrangements. It felt more like someone's living room. I had said I loved wildflowers and that Russ's color was purple. The casket looked like it was surrounded by a purple glow.

I had lived with my goodbye for two days, but now many said their goodbyes for the first time. I was comforted by the presence of so many people and by the opportunity to talk and share so openly about Russ and his memories.

We cried at the wake and then came back to the house and drank as we laughed and remembered Russ. We were Italian, but if felt like a full-blown Irish wake. My brother boarded the plane after a late night and had brought his tuxedo pants by mistake. That small, silly thing was enough to give us a good laugh in the midst of the sadness.

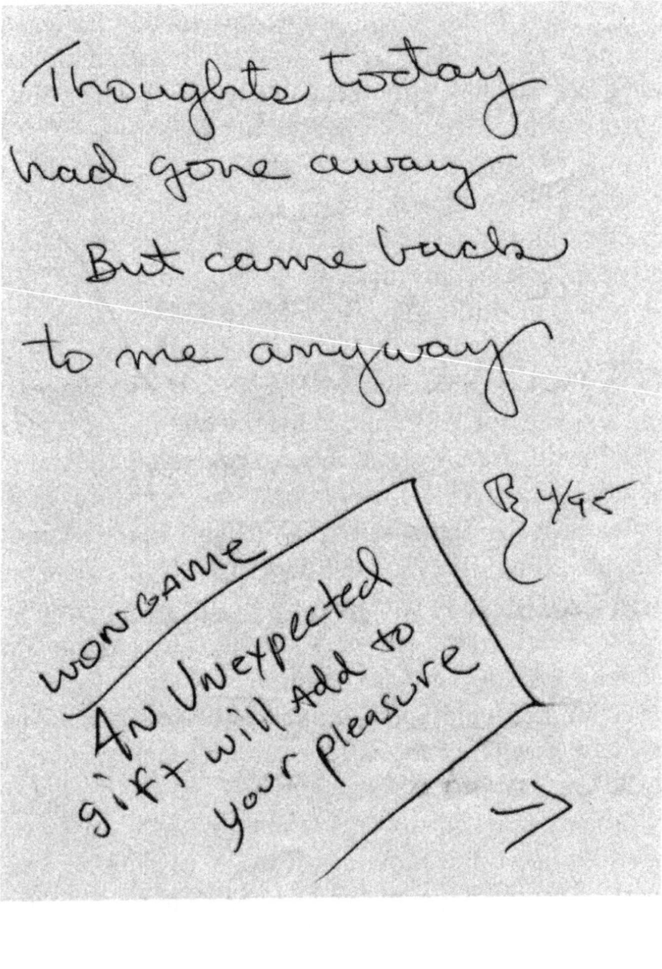
Thoughts today
had gone away
But came back
to me anyway

4/95

WON GAME

An Unexpected
gift will Add to
your pleasure

Go Long

Louisa ~ December 14, 2002

I waited with my family outside the church for the funeral procession to begin. People stopped to give me a quick hug. I was so touched by so many who entered the doors. All the people who loved us gathered in one place.

His ultimate frisbee friends formed an honorary pallbearer line which preceded the casket, followed by his closest friends walking in with the casket. My immediate family and Russ's family followed the casket inside. We entered to the song "O Come all ye Faithful." Christmas was two weeks away. We met on Christmas, and now I said goodbye at the same time of year.

My biggest concern that day was that the music would play on cue at the service and at the cemetery. I had chosen excerpts from Russ's writings to be read by John, and had put two of his poems in the funeral book. I leaned into my brother Rich and said, "I feel weird because I am not crying."

Rich said, "Don't worry, Steve is crying enough for the both of you." I glanced down at my brother and saw tears lining his face.

I didn't list the songs in the funeral booklet. I thought it would be better to let them be a surprise. John introduced them, saying, "Louisa has chosen Here Comes the Sun because Russ loved the Beatles, and What a Wonderful World because he gave her the song in a music box as a gift." The songs played beautifully and on cue.

Pastor Staats gave the homily. He spoke about Russ and his faith. "He was ready to go and be with God, even though he told me he would have liked to spend more time with Louisa."

The funeral procession headed out to the cemetery. Russ was in a white hearse. I wondered if the funeral directors did this because of his love for Elvis. I was in a limo with Russ's family. When gathered around the coffin, Pastor Staats asked us to join in singing Away in a Manager. He then said I wanted to share something as well.

I said, "Russ chose this cemetery because it faced the ASU football stadium. So to honor his Sun Devils, I am going to play the ASU Fight Song."

At the end of the song, his friend, Matt, grabbed a frisbee that was on top of the casket and said, "Mike, go long." It seemed the most natural thing to do to sail a frisbee across the beautiful green lawn cemetery. The sight of that frisbee was a defiance to death and a yes to the human spirit to still live on. Russ' impulsive friends created a magnificent, beautiful moment.

Gifts of Russ

Louisa

S hortly after Russ died, I met with a wise soul who knew there were many gifts to take forward in the midst of my heartbreak. We experienced a lifetime of love in a very short time, and our friendship was always in the background of our lives.

A journey through grief is a book unto itself. It has taken me a very long time to finish this book. Many people asked me why. Perhaps at a subconscious level, I know this book closes the chapter with him. I am filled with joy to know that his legacy and his writing will go on to encourage others.

The gift of his love is the greatest gift for me; and these gifts I have carried forth:

- Carpe Diem. His daily creed to "Seize the Day."
- Never Give Up.
- Be Kind. Lead with kindness and a smile.
- Be Playful. Never stop having a childlike wonderment with life. Have fun and play.
- Be Present. Be present to the beauty of nature. Russ would take my hand many times to bring my attention to the sunsets.

- Be Open. Be open and engage with others.
- Be Brave. Stare down your fears and your opponent… "cancer."

Indomitable Spirit

Ken & Norma Symmes, Parents

From the moment our fourth child took his first breath, we knew that he would be one of a kind! With his sparkling blue eyes, it was inevitable that we would name him Russell, as both his grandfathers were named Russell and both had blue eyes. Thus began the odyssey of a boy born on August 24, 1958 in Fort Leavenworth, Kansas – a boy who cared deeply for his family and friends and loved life.

Initially, we thought that it would be easy to put together a page of gifts, but it soon became evident that that would not be possible. There are just too many memories of things that Russ said or did that we could call "gifts." So we have decided that his indomitable spirit is the most significant gift that Russ gave us.

There are many instances we could cite wherein Russ's indomitable spirit was displayed during his first thirty-two years of life, but we won't. Instead, we will go to January 1992, when Russ was stricken with brain cancer at the age of thirty-three. During the next ten years, he underwent surgeries, radiation, and chemotherapy, valiantly fighting the cancer and refusing to give in. Russ gained considerable strength and happiness with Louisa, the love of his life, by his side. But in November 2002, shortly after his forty-fourth birthday, he was struck anew. This cancer proved to be inoperable, and on December 11th he left us to be "with the Angels."

Almost every day, Mom and I recall something that Russ said or did that make us laugh or perhaps a little sad. We will always love him and cherish his indomitable spirit!

Love and Support

Steven Symmes, Brother

Russ's gift to me has always been his love and support. Even as an "obnoxious" little brother, he always stuck by my side and was there for his family and friends.

One of my best memories of Russ is the "sausage tree incident" in Hawaii. There was a tree that grew long pods that looked like giant sausages. Russ and I pondered what was inside these sausages, so one day we decided to find out. Being the older brother, I got to climb the tree; from the ground, Russ pointed out the biggest of the lot; it was almost two feet long. As it turned out, these sausages were not so easy to pick and were really, really heavy.

As I tugged and twisted the sausage, Russ kept cheering me on. Well, that sausage finally came free, dropped like a rock, and took me along with it. Let's just say I did not bounce; my foot immediately started to swell, but after all we had gone through we agreed we would carry it home. We didn't get far before I was ready to give up. That sausage must have weighed twenty pounds or more.

Russ said he would carry it home. The sausage was half his size back then and was probably half his weight, too. I can still see Russ with his arms wrapped around our prize. We started to walk home, with me hobbling behind. But Russ never complained and he encouraged me to keep up. To this day, I have no clue how he was able to get that thing home.

Later that day, we took a hack saw and cut up the sausage. We were a bit disappointed to find that the inside was solid and kind of smelled funny; but we now knew what was in it and I never had to climb a sausage tree again!

Family

Marjie Symmes, Sister-In-Law

There are no words to describe the many gifts that Russell gave: love, laughter, understanding, and most importantly what a real family is.

Steve and I had only known each other for six weeks when we traveled to Sierra Vista to meet Steve's parents and his family. I was a nervous, shy, wreck and had never been away from my family for a holiday before. We arrived late on Christmas Eve, and I was welcomed with open arms by all.

Christmas morning came, and somehow or other the Symmes family had figured out a way to get me Christmas presents – which I treasure to this day! We opened our presents and shared them one at a time with the rest of the family; then came Russell's turn. Karen had purchased a new shirt for Russell, who at this time was a buff football player. We jokingly called his shirt "Omar's tent." I had come from a very, very strict family and was not prepared for what happened next! Russell, in all of his wonderful shyness, dropped his jeans to try on his new shirt, very successfully mooning all of us. I turned as red as an apple while the rest of the family died of laughter at my reaction!

I soon became a member of this amazing family and became very familiar with the "moon." From that Christmas day on, when Russell saw me he always mooned me. We still have a picture of him mooning us, and we still miss the butt print on the window of the car! We have a sun and a moon at our front door because Russell made the sun rise and he still moons us every day.

Thank you, Russell, for being Russell.

Magic, Presence And Joy

Ryan Shwayder, Nephew

I think about Uncle Russell often. He was that favorite uncle that only exists in movies: fun, kind, inspirational, and way cooler than your parents.

Every time I go to put our name in at a restaurant, I remember him. He used to just walk up and start talking to everyone, brightening their day. He had a certain magic about his presence that could only be experienced, not explained.

He made kids feel welcome around the adults. Even if he was doing something you couldn't directly participate in, you felt included in his presence.

When I need to turn on the charm and act social, I emulate his behavior but I can never capture his same energy. It's not something you can fake. He cared about people and lit up every room he entered.

What I remember about him most is that he brought the joy of a dozen lifetimes in his abbreviated visit to this world. Russell's gift was that Russell was gifted to us.

Funny and Lighthearted

Brandt Shwayder, Nephew

It's going to be difficult to put into words some of what my uncle instilled upon me in his time on this planet. I will sum it up this way: my son Milo's middle name is Russell. It will serve as a reminder of the goodness of this man, and my hopes that my son will in some way share in his spirit and carry it forth into the world.

The one thing I can say for certain about Uncle Russell (as we called him) is that I only have good memories of him. He made time to be with each of us and take interest in whatever we were interested in. He was probably the kindest, funniest, most tenacious, and simply the most magnetic person I've ever known. Everyone was drawn to him, and he was the coolest guy I ever knew!

He set an example to live by, always funny and always lighthearted – something I think we all can learn from.

Power of a Smile

Jamie Shwayder, Niece

Russ was one of my favorite people in the whole world. He had this way of walking into a room and making everyone smile, laugh, and feel like they were one of his old friends. He had such a spirit about him. And at 6'6", he made quite an entrance everywhere he went!

Just before Thanksgiving, my mom and I went to visit Uncle Russ in Arizona. When we arrived at the house, I realized that the Uncle Russ I remembered didn't seem quite like himself. At that time, he was using a cane, was partially paralyzed on one side of his body, and was finding it harder and harder to speak. While he still had that same Uncle Russ spark in his eye, I wanted to see him smile like he used to.

That's when it dawned on me: Christmas. He and I both love Christmas time! We were more than a month away from St Nick, and there weren't any decorations in sight. This can't be so! So, while mom and Russ caught up, I went into the garage, found a box marked "decorations," and proceeded to pull out all the bundles of lights I could find. I went outside to the front of the house and started stringing up lights around the tree; layering strands as high as I could reach (or jump). I couldn't wait to show him, and I hoped to see that Russ spark light up again! I walked back into the house and told him we had a surprise outside. My mom and I walked him out, holding him up on either side, his eyes closed. He wondered what in the world was going on!

As Mom and Russ stood right under the tree, we counted, "One... two... three!" On three, his eyes opened and I plugged in the lights. The whole tree lit up and shined like the sunrise! I was so excited. We laughed and smiled as I ran to give Uncle Russ a hug. He said many oohs, ahhhs, and wows, and I saw that Russ spark glistening with a few tears in his eyes.

We headed back inside, sat down, and started to wind down from the Christmas-y excitement. Uncle Russ looked at me and placed his hand on mine. Just when I thought he was about to say "Thank you," he said, "Jamie, never stop smiling that beautiful smile; you never know who might need it."

A few weeks later, Russ passed away. That was the last thing he ever said to me.

I didn't realize it then, but those final words would become my mantra. When I look at a stranger passing by, I smile. When I see my best friends or my family, I smile. When I'm having my hardest day, I still smile – because you never know who might need it.

Smiling at the world has pulled me out of my dark moments, lifted me higher in the best of moments, calmed me in times uncertainty and fear, and brought love into my life. The power of a smile is a power greater than I could ever imagine. I dare each of you to take this gift that Russ gave to me, and use it in your life every day. You never know what could be on the other side of a smile!

Positivity

Sue Shwayder, Sister

It's hard to pinpoint one thing as Russ's gift to me, but I think it would be his positivity. Every time I hear "It's a Wonderful World," I think of Russ. He always looked on the bright side of things. He was positive and loved life. Always adventurous, he made every minute count. He loved to laugh and tell jokes, and he made everybody feel special.

Of course, that was when he was an adult. As a kid, he was an annoying bundle of energy who never slowed down or shut up. I remember paying him with my babysitting money to be quiet and sit still. He was a fun brother, though, and I wish he were still here to bring light to everyone's life. Love you, Russ.

Love

Colleen Myers, Niece

Uncle Russell. He was one of a kind. It's almost impossible to put into words what an amazing person he was and how much he continues to touch lives.

As a young girl, I always idolized Uncle Russell. He made a lasting impression on everyone he met and was always the shining light in the room. I know that he made a big impact on my life. To this day, I talk to him as if he is still here. A part of me knows he is watching over all of us.

I remember on a family vacation when I was little, he gave me a twisty tie that was made into a ring. To this day, I remember how special it was to me. It was so special, I told my now husband, Chris, about it. In turn, when we were dating, he made me one, too. In some ways, Chris reminds me of Uncle Russell. That, to me, was home and a rare find. We named one of our twin boys Callum Russell to honor his memory. I was so blessed to have him in my life and witness what a true, kind, strong soul he was. For this, he will never be forgotten, but celebrated and loved forever.

Presence

Karen May, Sister

Every time I see a rainbow, I say, "Thanks, Russ," because I know it's his is way of saying "hello" from heaven. He touched many lives with his laughter, charm, and infectious smile. When we lived in Hawaii, I remember taking a picture of him sitting on the couch wearing a Hawaiian shirt and shorts, with dad's flip-flops on the wrong feet and dad's glasses perched on his nose, reading a newspaper upside down. He was always playing jokes, and shared his happiness and inner light with everyone he met.

As his big sister, I watched him grow from an impish little boy to a man who was always larger than life (all 6'6" of him). His blue eyes captured your attention, shining with mischief, love, and compassion. During a difficult time in my life, Russ was there to help me pick up the pieces, ensuring Tyler, Colleen, and I were safe and able to move forward. As he battled cancer, he never stopped believing in miracles. His faith, (and let us admit it, his stubbornness) helped him live a good life despite the odds. His unwavering love for his family, wife, and friends will embrace us forever.

Zeal for Life

Tyler May, Nephew

I am not what you would call a spiritual or religious person. Yet throughout each day, when I see a rainbow traversing the sky, or narrowly avoid an accident or injury, hear a Beatles song, encounter anything related to Hawaii, feel depressed, or enjoy a moment of mirth, an undeniably angelic presence fills my heart and mind. Russell's kind yet playful eyes and his warm, knowing smile flash before me. His mellow, caring voice whispers to me. His zeal for life, no matter how unfair or painful it could be, inspires me to move forward when I want to run away. I may not believe in angels, but I do believe in Russell.

Carpe Diem (Seize The Day)
Blaine Tubbesing, Friend

Carpe Diem. Seize the Day. A simple thought, but one with deep meaning. We know not what tomorrow holds for us. There are no guarantees.

One day, you could be the picture of health; the next, you could be having a grand mal seizure in France. One day, you could be the owner of a successful business with a beautiful wife and a spectacular home; the next, you could be a greeter at a fitness center, divorced and living with your old roommate.

When you are diagnosed with cancer, there are many options as to what action, if any, you take next.

Some choose to do nothing and to let life take its course. Others seek out the best cancer doctors in the world in hopes of finding a cure and extending their lives. It is the rare person, though, that chooses to make the most out of each and every day, doing the most they can for others.

Russ was that rare person. He did not give up on life; he lived it. When the world-renowned Barrow Neurological Institute performed his brain surgery, Russ did not cross his fingers and hope for the best. He willingly took on the challenge of counseling other future Barrow's patients with the same rare cancer he had. He could speak first-hand of what the experience was like. He was not empathizing with them; he was encouraging them. He was not just thinking of himself; he was concerned about others who were facing the same challenge in life.

The doctors told him that he had three months to live. He lived over ten years with his cancer. He worked in the movie industry as a key grip, he remarried a beautiful woman (both inside and out), and he once again lived in a beautiful home. He never gave up; he taught me by example how to seize the day. Carpe Diem, Kahuna.

216

ACKNOWLEDGMENTS

The pages of this book traveled from piles to files to binders, hidden away in closets and storage units for years. All along the way, Russ' parents, Ken and Norma Symmes; and his siblings, Karen, Sue, and Steven gave me encouragement when I took giant steps. And grace in the silence of the years when I took no action.

The generosity of so many helped me cross the line to completion. My first book coach, Tom Bird who called me a writer. Jeff Del Nero took it from the page to the computer. He tirelessly scanned hundreds of poems, narratives, and pictures. He created the first cover. The book lay dormant for the next five years, until Chris Baker lit the next fire. He helped me enter every poem and graphic into a new format. Jacob Shaver helped me edit many parts of my story. I was so close, yet so far. Two years later, the generosity of Eric Riesenberg took the copy to another level.

In 2019, I entered a program called Heartcore Leadership. There, I declared that I would finish the book. I owe a special shout out to Curtis Jackson, who role played "Russ," and helped me know that I was ready to close this chapter. Curtis and HCL 8, your clearing of joy, authenticity, power, connection, and love made this finally possible.

I interviewed many people to take me to the finish line. A special thanks to Shanda Trofe with Transcendent Publishing, Kim Eldredge with New Frontier Books and Editor, Holly Doherty.

Thank you to the many friends – too many to mention – who encouraged me to finish this book. I do have code names for people to whom I would like to give a special shout out: Mystic, Dory, and Buttons. I can finally say, "Yes it's done."

Lastly, a special thank you to my parents, Richard and Amelia Percudani. I find it very hard to find the right words to honor you. I was blessed to be born to parents and an extended family that was filled with love, generosity, grace and a passion for living life to the fullest. My siblings – Carol, Richard, Stephen, and Paul – and their families are my comrades in courage, laughter, and possibility. I know that with you by my side, I can do anything.

ABOUT THE AUTHORS

Russell K. Symmes (Russ) was an entrepreneur in video, film production, and travel. He was diagnosed with a life-threatening brain tumor at the age of thirty-three and began writing poems after his diagnosis.

A recipient of the Editor's Choice Award for Outstanding Achievement in Poetry by The National Library of Poetry. He dedicated his life to help other newly diagnosed brain cancer patients through The Bloch Cancer Hotline.

Russ lived a life of adventure with his wife, Louisa, family, and many friends. He never missed an ASU football game. He was known by many as "The Big Kahuna," a nickname given while an offensive tackle for Arizona State University.

Louisa M. Percudani is an Emmy Award Nominated Television Producer, Coach, and Speaker. She is dedicated to the legacy of her husband Russ to give newly diagnosed or those living with cancer the encouragement to live now and never give up. Louisa is also a breast cancer thriver and is currently working on her soon to be released memoir. She loves to connect at louisapercudani.com.

Laura,

It is the night before we get married and I am here by myself thinking of the life you and I are beginning. I have never in my life felt better about my future. There is an angel here with me telling me about the years we have together, children and our incredible life we share.

I love you like I have never felt before. I can't wait until 11:30am.... when you read this we will be married.

Thank you GOD!

love,
your Husband Russ